WIL

FOLK
TALES

WILTSHIRE

FOLK TALES

KIRSTY HARTSIOTIS

The
History
Press

To my grandparents, Alexander Clark Smith and Mina Smith

First published 2011

Reprinted 2011, 2012, 2014, 2017

The History Press
The Mill, Brimscombe Port
Stroud, Gloucestershire, GL5 2QG
www.thehistorypress.co.uk

British Library Cataloguing in Publication Data.
A catalogue record for this book is available from the British Library.

ISBN 978 0 7524 5736 9

Typesetting and origination by The History Press
Printed in Great Britain by TJ International, Padstow, Cornwall

CONTENTS

ACKNOWLEDGEMENTS

I'd like to thank Valerie Dean, Fiona Eadie, Josie Felce, Miranda Holmes, Diana Humphrey, Austin Keenan, Chloe Lees, Temi Odurinde, David Phelps, Glenn and Mags Smith, and Jess Wilson for listening to Wiltshire stories *ad infinitum* and giving feedback. Swindon Library, Highworth Historical Society and the Swindon & Wiltshire History Centre have all offered invaluable help in tracking down information and facts. Special thanks go to my old colleagues at Swindon Museum & Art Gallery, Lydiard Park and the Richard Jefferies Museum for setting me on the Wiltshire path.

But most of all I'd like to say thank you to Anthony Nanson for all his help, encouragement and love on every step of the journey.

ILLUSTRATIONS

The cover illustration is by Katherine Soutar and illustrates the story 'The Raising of the Giant's Dance'. The map and the illustrations at the beginning of each story are by the author (© 2010). All other illustrations are from the Dover Pictorial Archive and are reproduced in accordance with their terms and conditions.

MAP OF THE STORIES

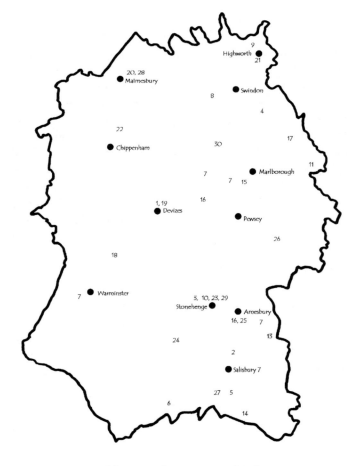

A map of the major places mentioned in the stories.

INTRODUCTION

I first came to Wiltshire at the age of thirteen while in the midst of a passion for all things Arthurian. It seemed to this East Anglian a very alien landscape, but I loved it. Wiltshire's rolling hills, its downlands, woods and waters seem to me liminal places. There is an eerie sense of the long ages that human beings have lived in this land. There are many spots where you might expect strange happenings and encounters. My time as a curator at a Wiltshire museum only heightened this sense that anything was possible here.

Wiltshire is a county at the centre of British history. From the very beginnings of culture in Britain the people living in what is now Wiltshire have made a significant impact on the rest of the country. The county has not only one but two of the largest and most important prehistoric ceremonial complexes in Europe. Stonehenge and Avebury are both UNESCO World Heritage sites and were of immeasurable importance to the people who built and used them. They are very much still in use today, not only by the Pagans who use them as places of worship, but also by the visitors who come to experience the religious sites of our ancestors.

Many stories about King Arthur are set in Wiltshire. In this book are no less than four stories about King Arthur and those who came before and after him (Nos 3, 10, 16 and 25). The enchanter Merlin is even said to be buried at Marlborough. In Saxon times Wiltshire was at the heart of the kingdom of Wessex, which would soon go on to form the core of England. Chippenham and Wilton were two of King Alfred the Great's palaces, and his great victory against the Vikings in AD 878 is thought to have taken place at Edington, near Westbury.

In more recent years, Wiltshire has been renowned for its wool and its great cathedral at Salisbury. In the nineteenth century Swindon became the hub of the south-west's railway network, Brunel's Great Western Railway. The Swindon Works is one of the most significant Victorian engineering works in the world; it provided amenities for its employees that inspired the National Health Service and the network of public libraries. It has been proposed as another UNESCO World Heritage site. Less gloriously, perhaps, Wiltshire can also lay claim to be the place where tobacco was first smoked in Britain – at South Wraxall manor house by Sir Walter Raleigh and his host Sir Walter Long, who features in one of the stories in this book (No. 22).

The county has been known as 'Wiltshire' – or 'Wiltunscire' – since at least the ninth century, and a shire resembling the modern county probably existed since at least the seventh century. In the late twentieth and twenty-first centuries administrative boundaries have changed, but that only means that it is more crucial today than ever to celebrate the county that came into being more than 1,000 years ago.

The stories in this book come from many different sources. Many of the stories are from the ordinary people of Wiltshire, stories they told to entertain, warn and teach each other. We are lucky in Wiltshire, however, that there has been a tradition of collecting stories since the Middle Ages.

The first collector, William of Malmesbury, was born in the late eleventh century. He was a monk at Malmesbury Abbey. Inspired by reading the eighth-century Northumbrian historian Bede, William wrote two histories, *Deeds of the English Kings* (c. 1120, revised 1127) and *Deeds of the English Bishops* (1125). His tales range far wider than his native Wiltshire, but he features many local events and draws on the history of his own monastery. He is regarded today as one of England's most celebrated medieval chroniclers.

The next, Geoffrey of Monmouth, was, as his name suggests, probably born in Wales in around 1100. He may have been of

Welsh, Breton or even Norman ancestry. It is thought that his father's name was Arthur, and Geoffrey may have heard the popular Breton and Welsh tales of King Arthur as a small child. He too became a monk and seems to have spent most of his life in Oxford. He is best known for his book *The History of the Kings of Britain* (c. 1136). Unlike William of Malmesbury's largely historical tales of English kings and bishops, Geoffrey's book is a rollicking saga of Britain's legendary heroes. It tells the story of the Matter of Britain; the story of King Arthur. Several of the tales are set in Wiltshire, and it is Geoffrey who brings familiar landmarks like Stonehenge into the story for the first time. He started a tradition of Wiltshire Arthurian stories. Even Sir Thomas Malory, who wrote *Le Morte d'Arthur* in the fifteenth century, sets Queen Guinevere's death in the county.

In the seventeenth century another local man became interested in collecting Wiltshire lore. John Aubrey, also from near Malmesbury, was a great collector of information on every subject from geology to society gossip to folklore. He mapped the megaliths at Avebury for the first time and discovered a series of pits at Stonehenge that date to the earliest phase of the monument: the Aubrey Holes. He was fascinated by his own county and many of his works touched on its traditions, including *A Natural History of Wiltshire*. He started a *History of Northern Wiltshire* (incomplete at his death in 1697), and several Wiltshire monuments feature in his *magnum opus*, *Monumenta Britannica*. Aubrey didn't achieve recognition for his scholarship during his lifetime and most of his work went unpublished. Today, however, we recognise him to be a pivotal figure in many subjects from archaeology to folklore.

In the late nineteenth and early twentieth century, two great collectors and tale-spinners arose at opposite ends of the county. Edward Slow was a coach and wagon builder in his native Wilton. He is best known for his humorous verse that captures the Wiltshire dialect he was keen to preserve. He wrote for the ordinary people of Wiltshire and often pokes fun at authority. But he was keenly aware that an old way of life was dying out and, like Richard Jefferies and W.H. Hudson, he set out to record it.

The other was Alfred Williams the 'Hammerman Poet'. Williams was from South Marston, in the north of the county, and worked at the Swindon Railway Works. He taught himself literature and several languages at the Mechanics Institute and at home. He started writing at the age of twenty-one, and five years later had published his first collection of poetry. Another four followed. But he also collected tales from his local area, starting with South Marston, then ranging out on his bicycle to take in many other villages. He produced three books on village lore, and the definitive collection of folk songs from north Wiltshire.

Kathleen Wiltshire compiled the first comprehensive set of folk tales for the county in the 1960s. Her work was followed by that of Ralph Whitlock, John Chandler, Katy Jordan and many others.

In this book I have tried to provide a diverse range of stories, from high legends of King Arthur to the tales of ordinary people, and also include some of the great moments in history that took place in this county. Some tales are humorous, some are tragic – some are even true! And some evoke an otherworldly Wiltshire, the Wiltshire of dreams, and of the fair folk.

I treated the stories exactly as I would any other tale I want to tell. When you work up a story to tell, your starting point can be anything from a long, fully developed narrative, to a series of historical facts or a tiny snippet of information about a place or person. You must first make the story your own. I strip the tale down to the bare bones and then build it up again by adding flesh until the story is ready to be told.

I have explored the county from top to toe while researching this book. Where possible I visited the site of the story and followed the journeys of the characters. Many of the stories relate to the land itself, explaining landscape features, warning against disturbing the peace, or telling of encounters with the fair folk, ghosts and strange beasts that haunt the county and the wider British landscape.

Every hill, valley, river and road has – or had – a tale behind it. Once, it was likely that people knew all the stories of their locality, but in our modern world, where people are unlikely to stay in one place all their lives and have many other stimuli from television, the internet and travel, we are more likely to know the stories of our favourite films and television programmes than the stories of the place in which we live. It is my hope that this book, like the others in this series, will help to revive that local knowledge. The book is in no way exhaustive; there is far more Wiltshire lore out there than can fit in these pages, and it is evolving all the time. Have you heard, for example, about the crop circles or the radioactive rabbits? It gives me incalculable pleasure as I travel through the county to say to myself (or my long-suffering partner), 'This is where the maid found the maggot' or 'Here is where Squire Parker met the stag'. I hope the stories will give you a taste of that pleasure, and encourage you to tell them to others and go out and discover more stories for yourself.

1

THE MOONRAKERS

Ikey Perritt, the landlord of the Pelican in Devizes, was out of brandy. He had plenty of cider, ale and barley wine, but the fine French brandy was all gone and Christmas was coming. Now, the price of French brandy would have made any Lord and Lady Muck wince, especially in those straitened times. Perritt and his customers were not rich men. But Perritt was used to getting a good price, and he had his regular suppliers. One of them, a fellow Devizes man by the name of James Chapman, had promised him a delivery a good month ago, but there had been no word since. Perritt decided that it was time that he paid Chapman a visit.

When he reached Chapman's house he knocked on the door. Chapman answered himself, and looked horrified to see him.

'Christ! You can't show your face here! What if someone saw you? Quick, get inside.' Perritt was hustled through the door and sat down. A glass of ale was pressed into his hand, and then Chapman took a deep breath. 'You'll be here about the brandy,' he said. 'Well, that's fair enough. And it's here alright, been here a good three weeks, but I've had a right do getting it here, I can tell you.

'I'd met up with one of my old contacts, old Mabett, from Tilshead way. He had a few kegs he'd bought off a Southampton man, and I'd a few I'd bought off a man from Romsey. We figured that between us we'd have you supplied all the way through till Lent, with that lot!

'So off we went to Southampton, and I had a plan for a smooth journey home. We had a cart and a donkey, and we loaded the barrels up onto the cart and lashed them down. Then we covered the whole lot with hay, and tied that down too. Then, for verisimilitude, I got a spade and a shovel and a couple of old hay rakes and strapped them on the side of the cart. Then we dressed ourselves up in a pair of farmer's smocks, cross gartered our trouser legs and slapped broad-brimmed straw hats on our heads. We didn't quite go as far as chewing a piece of straw, but we would have done – for verisimilitude.

'We'd chosen our night carefully, a bleak 'un, cloudy and with a few spits and spots of rain; the kind of night that a body would be happy to cosy up by the fire with a glass of toddy in his hand. A fine night for smuggling! So off we set, going at as fast a clip as the donkey would let us.

'It was easy going through the forest out of Southampton, under cover of the trees and the darkness. We knew the first test would be on Cranborne Chase. We crept out onto the open ground and set us along the rides. In our attire, we couldn't have looked less like poachers, but the foresters wouldn't have given a fig – you should see them, Ikey, with their basket armour woven by their loving wives, and their broad woven helmets and their cudgels ready to whack a poacher and send him straight to jail. But the clouds stayed low, there was no one about and we were soon up at the Wiltshire Coppice. Home and dry – or so we thought.

'We moved steadily across the Downs, heading north, over the Nadder, past the woods at Fonthill, getting closer to home. But by now the night was changing. The drizzle was long gone, the clouds were breaking up and we could see the full moon high above the hills, with the clouds scudding fast across it. I'd forgotten it was full moon – I'll not forget again.

'There was no one out that night. I'd have called it uncanny, if it hadn't been so convenient. But by now the clouds were all gone, and the full moon lit the way and made for easy travelling. We pressed on, and we were so nearly home – so nearly! We were here in Devizes. We'd snuck up by St James', using the churchyard and trees for cover and we were just skirting the Crammer pond when the donkey froze.

'We froze as well, looking around for what might have frightened it, but there was nothing to be seen. Mabett was all of a pother. He leapt off the cart and was whacking at the donkey and hissing at it to go on, but the cussed beast wouldn't shift, just dug its heels in more.

'"Mabett," says I, "stop it now. You'll only make it yell." And sure enough, the donkey was soon bellowing away and I was sure that the excisemen – and every man, woman and child in the town – would find us and our brandy. "Stop it. Stop it," I cried, but the donkey had the last laugh.

'As Mabett brought his switch down hard on the beast's back, it kicked out, bucking up and kicking the traces of the cart right off. The cart upended, and hay, rakes and shovels were scattered all over the ground. For a moment the kegs held, and then they rolled out as well, straight into the pond.

'We were cussing and swearing, I can tell you, but in we waded as the damn things bobbed up and down in the water, and we tried to roll them out. But no sooner were we in the pond, than we heard the sound of a horse's hooves pounding along Church Walk towards us. Mabett and I looked at each other – it must be an exciseman! But I had a plan.

'"Get those rakes, and a wisp o' straw," says I, "and I'll push the barrels into the reeds. Now, when he gets here, you just get that rake and start raking at the water – just there – and leave the talking to me."

It was the exciseman, sure enough, and he brought his horse right up the edge of the pond. "Night poachers!" he began. "And if you aren't, I swear I'll eat my hat!" Then he stopped and seemed to see for the first time what we were doing.

'"Oh zur," says I in my very best Wiltshire, chewing away on my wisp o' straw for verisimilitude, "we beant no poachers, bit 'av' 'ad a' mishap, as ya zee – tha' donk mead a zudden start – he gied a kick, and out went oor things, which lays all about – an' look – thur's oor gurt yeller cheese. He rolled straite into the pond – and so we're reakun 'im out agin!"

The exciseman stared at us a minute, raking away at the bright white disc on the water, and then he burst out laughing.

'"You fools," he said. "Can't you see? That's no cheese. It's the reflection of the moon – look, can't you see it shining above you?"

But we didn't look; we just kept on raking at the white and shining thing in the pond till he nearly burst his sides with laughing.

'"That beats it all clean," he cried, "to see you crazy idiots raking at the moon!" And with that, he spurred his horse and rode away. As soon as he was gone, we rolled out the barrels from the reeds as quick as you like, got them back on the cart, covered them with hay and we were on our way, the donkey moving now as sweet as if butter wouldn't melt in its mouth.

'And that's why I've not delivered. I'm awaiting a cloudy, wet night so that we might sneak it all away.'

Perritt laughed long and loud at the story. Chapman flushed deep red and said, 'and I'll thank you to keep that story under your hat. If it gets out, we'll be the laughing stock of 'Vizes!'

Perritt gave his word, and soon enough the barrels of French brandy were safely ensconced in his cellar, no harm done after their dunking. But the story did get out. The exciseman couldn't resist and he told all his friends the tale. He was the toast of many a gathering so that the tale spread throughout the country and all of England knew for sure and certain that Wiltshire folk were fools. But at the Pelican Inn that Christmas, everyone raised a glass of the finest French brandy and toasted that exciseman who was taken in by a Wiltshire clown!

Smuggling tales are rife throughout Wiltshire. The county lies on the smuggling route between the South Coast and London. This story of locals playing on the assumption that country folk are foolish is first mentioned as far back as 1787, but I've taken my lead from the excellent poem, 'The Wiltshire Moonrakers' by Edward Slow and combined it with evidence that it was John Chapman of Devizes and Mr Mabett from Tilshead that did the deed. The location is also contentious. The original story is set in Cannings, but there was no pond or river in Bishop's or All Cannings at that time. Many people say that it took place in the Crammer in Devizes. In those days the Crammer was in the parish of Bishop's Cannings, so it might be true.

2

THE FLYING ARROW

Church and State were inextricably linked at Sarum. The cathedral and the fort nestled together within the walls of the castle. It must have seemed like a good idea at the time they were built, thirty years after the Norman Conquest, so soon after the English rebellions that followed.

However, the idea was a disaster from the word go. Only five days after the church was consecrated, the tower roof blew off. And it only got worse. The wind made such a racket that the monks could hardly hear themselves sing. There was hardly any water on the hill and the soldiers made sure the priests had to buy it at an inflated price from the farmers below. The church-builders hadn't provided enough rooms for the priests, so those had to be rented from the soldiers. As for the building, if it wasn't the tower roof blown off, then it was windows blown out or masonry tumbled by the ever-present wind.

For a century the priests put up with it, but in the early thirteenth century another problem arose. The soldiers had no respect for the priests and taunted them day and night. It was a bad time for England. King John had fought against everyone from the Pope down. Most of the kingdom's French lands were lost, taxes had shot sky high, his own barons had risen against him, and for long periods of his reign the whole country was excommunicated. The dead weren't buried, babies went unbaptised and sins weren't shriven. It didn't get any better when John died and his young son, Henry III, came to the throne.

The castle was controlled by William Longspée, King John's bastard half-brother. He was a good lord, but his loyalty to the Crown meant he was often away, fighting for the King. The castle grew unruly in his absence.

Matters came to a head on Rogation Sunday, 25 April 1219. The priests processed from the church, out of the castle and down to the bishop's lands below. The farmers and the green lads beat the bounds of the land, and the priests sang hymns and blessed it for another season. The bishop's lands were extensive and it was well after dark when the weary priests processed back up the hill to the castle. But when they reached the castle, they found the gates were locked.

They hammered on the doors. They shouted and screamed, but no one answered. They were forced to spend the night huddled against the castle walls with the beggars and tinkers and ladies of ill repute. It was a cold and scary night. Not a single one of the priests managed to get a wink of sleep.

The soldiers laughed when they let the priests in the next morning. They taunted them every time they dared emerge from the church. Bishop Poore decided that enough was enough. He wrote to the Pope, requesting permission to build a new cathedral

far away from the soldiers and the castle. The reply came by early summer. The Pope had granted him a licence to build. The question was: where?

The best land in the area belonged to Wilton Abbey. Founded by Alfred the Great after his battle against the Vikings in AD 871, the abbey had well-watered and abundant lands, full of crops, fruit and fat sheep. The bishop was the Abbess's superior. He could order her to give up her land.

Poore wasn't an ordering kind of man, so he set out on his donkey to beg the Abbess for a parcel of land. As he entered the town, he passed a row of cottages. Sitting outside were a group of old women, spinning and basking in the summer sunshine. They watched him go by. Then one of the old women, in the piercing voice of one whose hearing is starting to go, said, 'I do wonder at that bishop, that he comes to Wilton. Perhaps he means to marry the Abbess. Do you think he's got a dispensation?'

Bishop Poore flushed, but one of the other women shushed her and said, 'Don't be so silly! He's just off to ask her for some land to build that new church of his. Haven't you heard?'

The old woman turned to her friend in shock. 'Does the bishop not have any land of his own that he must rob the Abbess? God loves him not who grudges his own.'

The bishop hung his head in shame. The woman was right. He had to use his own lands. He turned the donkey around and went home.

That very night, the bishop had a dream the like of which he'd never had before. The Virgin Mary came to him and said, 'Bishop Poore, your new church and town will be blessed with peace and prosperity if you will do one thing for me. Build the church on land dedicated to me, and I will bless it.'

Bishop Poore woke up knowing what he had to do. He got out his rent books and his lists and scoured them from end to end, but not a single farm or field seemed to be named for the Virgin. So he went out into the fields and asked farmers and tenants, but nobody could help him. At his wits' end, the bishop wondered whether the Virgin had meant him to go to the nuns at Wilton and ask them.

He went out and walked his lands one last time before heading back to Wilton. He chanced upon two soldiers, slightly the worse for drink. They were casting bets to see who was the best archer, and the bishop stopped to listen.

'I bet you,' cried the first, 'I can shoot my arrow two fields away!'

'An' I bet you that you shoot it – bam – right at your feet!' cried the second.

The first archer drew back his bow and let fly the arrow, and it soared through the air. It landed just over the fence.

'Well,' said the first, 'let's see you do better!'

'I bet,' said the second, readying his bow, 'that I can get my arrow, not one, not two, but three fields away. See where that brindled cow is?'

He let fly the arrow and it landed close enough to the cow to spook it.

'That's it!' cried the second. 'All the way to Merryfield!'

'What did you say?' cried the bishop. 'What did you call that field?'

The two archers turned to him. 'Why,' said the first, 'that's Merryfield.'

The bishop clasped his hands together. Merryfield. Mary's Field. His prayers were answered. 'And whose land is it on?'

The two archers stared at him as if he were mad. 'Why, my lord,' said the second. 'It's your own land.'

The bishop fell down on his knees and gave thanks.

Work began at once. William Longspée and his wife Ela, perhaps contrite about the soldiers' usage of the priests, laid the foundation stones. The new cathedral at Salisbury was built very quickly, in only thirty-eight years. The priests were very keen to get down off that hill!

But William Longspée didn't live to see the building completed. He died only five years after the cathedral was begun. He'd been fighting in France for young King Henry. He was hale and hearty and speaking of his desire to see his wife and the work on the church. But he died five days after he arrived back in England, before he even got home to Salisbury. The rumour ran that he was poisoned by Herbert de Burgh, the King's regent, jealous of William's favour with Henry. So William had the dubious honour of being the first to be buried in the new church. In 1791 his tomb was opened and a rat was found lodged in his skull. It had died of arsenic poisoning.

Bishop Poore didn't live to see the church consecrated either, but he started work on improving the lot of the people of Salisbury. He opened a church school and promoted health and safety: every Sunday his priests preached that children should not be left alone in their houses with lit fires.

In 1228 his successes at Salisbury paid off and he was made Bishop of Durham, a very prestigious post. He died in 1237, content in the knowledge that not only had he done well in Durham but he had secured a fine future for Salisbury.

But what became of the old church still marooned on the hill of Sarum? Well, if you go into Salisbury's Cathedral Close today and look carefully at the stones, you'll find it in the walls and houses.

In another version of the story, the bishop himself fired the arrow that marked where the cathedral would be built. The arrow hit a deer, which then ran, and the place where the deer died became the new site. A more prosaic explanation for the site's name, Merrifield or Myrfield, is given by Edward Hutton in Highways and Byways in Wiltshire, *1919. He suggests that 'the site chosen was at the point of junction of the three ancient hundreds of Underditch, Alderbury and Cawdon, and was therefore called Maerfield or boundary field'.*

3

THE NIGHT OF THE
LONG KNIVES

When the Romans left, Britain was in turmoil as the petty chiefs struggled for the high kingship. Constantine leapt into the breach. He called himself Emperor, the third of that name, but he died young. He left three sons. The eldest, Constans, had been in a monastery since he was a boy, and the other two, Ambrosius Aurelianus and Uther Pendragon, were just children. The nobles despaired, but there was one who saw this as an opportunity. Vortigern, Lord of Wirtgernesburg, near Bath, said that Constans should rule. He was his father's eldest son, monastery taught or not. When the young man was brought to the throne, Vortigern was there, offering advice and counsel and nodding understanding as Constans stumbled through this unfamiliar world of warriors and politicians.

Constans came to a country already at war with the Picts in the north. As war raged, Constans was soon listening only to Vortigern. But it wasn't enough for Vortigern to have the ear of the King. He wanted to be king himself. He married Constans' mother, putting aside his first wife, the mother of his sons. He made a contract with the Picts, with silken promises and lies, and they sneaked into the fortress and murdered the young King. Ambrosius and Uther fled across the sea to Brittany and the friendly court of Budic I of Cornouaille, and the British nobles did nothing as Vortigern declared himself High King over them all.

But that was only half the story. While Vortigern ruled from his Wiltshire castle, and the British nobles plotted and schemed to overthrow him in their decaying villas, a group of desperate men hauled their three ships up on a beach on the Isle of Thanet in Kent. All unknowing, they had fled to a land about to sink into fierce war. If they had known they would not have changed their course, for they were warriors, every one.

When Vortigern heard that strangers had landed, he recognised an opportunity and set off to Kent. When he arrived on the flat sands he saw the ships pulled up, their prows fierce with toothed dragons, and an encampment of men huddled around a fire with a banner emblazoned with a white horse snapping in the wind above them. Their clothes were strange to him, but when one stood up to greet him, Vortigern saw something in him he recognised. This fierce blond warrior, his plaited hair shot with the first streaks of grey, had as much naked ambition as Vortigern himself. The man stepped forward. His eyes were bold.

'I am Hengist,' he said, then gestured to a man behind him. 'This is my brother, Horsa. We have come from far away to your shore to ask for sanctuary. In my land there is famine, and in such times of hardship, the young men of good family take themselves away to find new lands. No longer will we ride across the plains of Saxony – we come to throw ourselves at your mercy, great lord.'

Vortigern liked the man's words, but more than that, he saw the gleaming weapons, the bulging muscles. He saw something that would give him an edge over the British nobles. Holding out his hand, he said, 'Join with me and you will have land here. You and your men will fight as my bodyguards and earn honour and glory on the battlefield!'

The men gave a ragged cheer, but Vortigern didn't notice a small smile play across Hengist's lips.

'Oh yes,' said Hengist, 'we will join you, High King. We will be right by your side.'

With his new fighting force, Vortigern soon pushed back the rebel Picts. The British nobles were awed by the new army and Vortigern gained power. He went back to Wiltshire to sit in comfort in his castle. But back on Thanet, more and more Saxons poured into Britain, bringing their families and starting to work the land there. Hengist's own young daughter, Rowena, was among them. Hengist began to make plans.

He invited Vortigern to a feast to celebrate the building of his palace on Thanet. Vortigern was impressed by the great structure with its steeply pitched roof and the crossed horse-head gable high above the door. He was impressed by the pillared hall, and the cauldron hanging over the fire in the centre of the room, but more than anything he was impressed by Rowena as she stepped into the room holding the mead-horn high. Her blond hair rippled down her back and her blue eyes glinted, and he could see all her young curves through her clinging gown. As she poured the mead into his cup she whispered soft words in her own tongue.

'She says, "Hlaford King, wes hail" – Lord King, your good health!' cried Hengist. 'It is our tradition – you must reply "Drinc hail" so we will have good health and prosperity!'

How could Vortigern not reply? He toasted the girl, and all night his eyes followed her as she poured drinks for the men.

They were wed soon after. Vortigern put aside Constantine's widow and married the fresh young Saxon girl. Soon, Hengist was at his side, day-in, day-out, as a treasured advisor, and more Saxons came and settled in the south-east, where the Romans had once settled their ancestors. The eastern coast became once more a Saxon shore.

The British looked at their King, and saw that he loved the Saxons above all others. Vortimer, the King's eldest son, saw a second woman in his father's bed who was not his mother. It was too much. Vortimer declared against his father, and once again Britain plunged into war.

At first the Saxons supported the High King, but Vortigern soon showed he couldn't fight everyone at once. What's more, he was rattled by a prophecy of defeat given by a young man with magical talents.

Hengist went to Horsa and said, 'This is our time, brother. This land is fine and fat with cattle and sheep. The crops spring from the ground ripe and glossy, and those dark women are witches in the sack. The King is afraid and snatching at shadows. The British are weak and would sooner fight against themselves than live in peace. Now is our time to act.'

The Saxons turned against Vortigern, and the whole country was consumed by war. The British despaired. They couldn't defeat the Saxons. Vortimer was only interested in pursuing his exhausted father, who fled further and further into the west, abandoning Wirtgernesburg. There had to be another way for peace.

A lone messenger was sent to Hengist's camp. 'My lords, I have been sent by the British lords to ask for a parley to end this senseless bloodshed. They ask you to meet with them on Salisbury Plain. All will stand in a circle of unity, Briton beside Saxon, Saxon beside Briton. There will be no weapons. They hope that through clever words a peace might be wrought between our peoples so we can share the land we both love.'

Hengist agreed, but as the messenger left he didn't see the small smile play across Hengist's face. Hengist called his men together. 'Men, these British bring us opportunities with open hands. We will go, but we will take our seaxes, our long knives. Tuck them into your boots, and when I give the signal, "Nemet seaxes!" take your seax and cut the throat of the man beside you!'

They gathered on the plain, the country rolling into woodland and grassland all around them and not a house or farm for miles. The Britons came, with their hair limed into spikes, and gold sparkling at their throats. The Saxons came, their long hair caught in plaits, gold glinting at their shoulders. Side by side they stood among the flickering torches and watched the sun set. It was hard to see who was a Briton and who was Saxon. Horses whickered in the fading light, and then, from out of nowhere, a voice cried, 'Nemet seaxes!'

The Britons fought back as best they could, but they had acted in good faith and had not brought their weapons. By the end of the night the flower of the British nobility lay dead on Salisbury Plain.

Initially Hengist seemed unstoppable. At the first battle he was victorious, and at the second and the third. But in the fourth battle, at Aylesford in Kent, his brother was slain and the battle lost. After the battle Hengist went out to retrieve the body himself. He stood with his brother cradled in his arms and searched the land for a place to lay him to rest. And there on a low hill, gleaming in the dying light, he saw a great white stone.

He laid his white horse banner over the stone and buried Horsa beside it. Hengist closed his eyes on the sorry cluster of men that remained with him. Although there were no torches lit in case the Britons found them, the quiet murmur of the scop took him away to how it should be. The lines of torches running down to the sea; the women singing; the great horse-prowed ship waiting to receive Horsa with all his treasure around him, and he, his brother, ready to cast him out onto the waves on his last voyage. He would not cry in front of his men, but inside he bled.

His men scattered and Hengist found himself on the run. He had no heart for the fight now his beloved brother was dead. As he crossed Salisbury Plain he saw the low mound raised to house the dead from what the Britons called the Night of the Long Knives. He felt all that he had done press on him, and as the Downs stretched out before him, he cowered in this alien land. Had he been wrong? Was this not the land for his people? He pressed further into the smooth rippling hills, riding hour after hour until he could go no further. As darkness fell he came to a scoured and ridged hill. He fell to his knees and, all alone, he begged Woden to send him a sign. Then, exhausted, he fell into a deep sleep.

When he awoke the sun was high, casting deep shadows onto the hill. Nothing was any different to how it had been the night before, and his shoulders sank. Above, a gull shrieked, and he looked up. There, ahead of him, cut into the chalk of the hill itself was his family's symbol – a horse. It was faded, and obscure, but plain enough for those with eyes to see.

'Thank you,' he whispered.

He was reunited with his men and they gathered together to fight one last time, and the battle was fought and won. Afterwards, Hengist took his men back to the hill, and they re-cut the white horse so that it gleamed in the sunlight. The Saxons were here to stay.

The story of the Night of the Long Knives comes from Geoffrey of Monmouth. William of Malmesbury suggests that Vortigern had a fort at Wirtgernesburg, modern Bradford-on-Avon. It was John Aubrey, another Malmesbury boy, who had the idea that the Uffington White Horse was cut by Hengist (whose name means 'stallion') in memory of his brother Horsa (whose name means 'horse'). We know the Uffington horse is much older than that, probably dating from the Bronze Age, so I decided to have Hengist re-cutting the horse instead.

4

STONE SOUP

Liddington was a poor village that year. The harvest had failed and the previous winter had been hard, with lambs and ewes dying, and this winter was worse. It had been a thin Christmas, a thinner January, and everyone knew the meaning of hunger. Belts were tightened and tempers frayed. So when the tinker walked in with pots and pans jingling from his pack, maybe it wasn't surprising that people slammed their doors in his face.

'You think we've money to waste on your rubbish?' cried the women of the village when he knocked on their doors and offered his wares.

The tinker shrugged his shoulders each time, gave a tug of his cap and moved on. It was the same at every door. He didn't sell anything. By now, it was getting dark and there was a taste of snow in the air. The tinker looked down the road towards Wanborough and the one towards Coate. He drew his coat closer round his neck as the wind blew and the first flakes fell. He nodded to himself, and turned back into the village. He tried the Sun and he tried the Bell, but they told him they never took in travelling folk and spat on the ground as he left. So he was back to knocking on doors again.

'Sleep here the night and risk our daughters in their beds? Risk our stock in the sheds? Be gone with you, and good riddance!' cried the women, as they slammed their doors on him again.

At last the tinker reached the final house in the village on the way to Coate, and he realised he hadn't knocked on this door at all. The building was so ramshackle that he had thought it derelict, but now that night had fallen he could see a light at the window. He hitched his pack higher on his back and knocked. An old woman, bent and lined, opened the door and stared at him.

'You'd better come in,' she said. 'It looks fierce out there.'

It was warm inside, if only because the room was so small. Gratefully, the tinker shrugged the pack from his back and looked around. A small fire flickered in the hearth. Drawn up beside it were a low stool and table. On the table sat a wooden bowl with the remains of a thin gruel stuck to the sides. A curtained area on the other side of the fire no doubt contained the old woman's bed. The lack of trinkets told a tale of poverty. There were no hanging herbs or vegetables, and few enough pots and pans.

'You can sleep by the fire,' the old woman said. 'But I can't offer you any food. I've none to give you, for I've just had the last of the winter oats.'

'Don't you worry, old mother,' said the tinker. 'As long as you have water and a big cooking pot, I'll cook you a meal fit for an Emperor. Stone soup.'

He bent down and opened up his pack, tumbling all his wares on the floor. From the very bottom he drew out a stone. It was grey and smooth with one bold white stripe running through it. The old widow knew enough to see it wasn't a local stone. Round Liddington, it would be flint – the curse of the farmer – Devil's toenails, shepherd's crowns and snakestones.

The widow ducked outside and came back a few minutes later with an old cauldron.

'From when I was a wife and my children were all with me. I never use it now they're all gone.' They chased out the spiders, carefully put a nest of mice back in the shed outside, and the widow gave it a brisk dust and scrub. Then she took her pail to fetch water from the well. When she got there, she found the blacksmith's wife, Farmer Boulter's wife and the rest, shivering as they drew up the water. As soon as they saw her, they gathered round.

'You took in the tinker! He'll murder you in your bed!'

The widow shook her head. 'He said he'll make me a meal fit for an Emperor. Stone soup!'

Now the villagers were intrigued. If you could make a soup out of stones then no one need ever go hungry again. So they followed the old widow back to her cottage and crowded around as the tinker made his preparations. First he placed the stone at the bottom of the pan, then he filled the pan with water and set it to boil on the fire.

It was a long wait, and stomachs were grumbling by the time it boiled. But instead of ladling it out, the tinker simply dipped a spoon in and tasted the hot liquid. He nodded and smacked his lips, and the village women craned closer.

'It's good,' he said. 'Fit for a cottar, perhaps. But to make it truly lordly a little bitty bit of onion wouldn't go amiss.'

There was a silence, and then the old widow said, 'I might have one – just the one – in the shed.' She hurried back outside and

returned with a sad and <u>wizened o</u>nion. The tinker just smiled and shucked off the skin, chopped up the rest and slung it in, and then gave the brew a good stir.

After a while, he tested it again. 'Well and good,' he said, licking his lips. 'That's pretty fine now, but to make it really lordly it could do with a bit of a root – maybe a carrot or a turnip?'

There was another silence, and then Farmer Boulter's wife cleared her throat, and admitted she might have one or two at home. She hurried out, and after a few minutes came bustling back in with some soft carrots, and into the pot they went.

After a while, the tinker tested the soup again, and again he smacked his lips. 'Getting wonderful fine now, but a little potato would improve it.' It was the blacksmith's wife who spoke this time, softly saying they had a few left. They were chopped and in the pot as soon as she brought them. As the village women watched, the stone soup began to thicken. The tinker tested it again.

'Coming along well,' he said. 'Pretty lordly, I'd say, but maybe a wee bone would make all the difference – would make it fit for a king.'

There was a longer silence this time, as most of the villagers could hardly remember when there had last been meat on the table. But eventually Farmer Tilley's wife admitted that they'd lost a sheep just a week ago. They'd butchered and sold it, but she'd held back a couple of bones, still with the marrow in, for the children. The tinker smiled as she hurried out into the night to fetch one, and kept on smiling as he added it to the pot.

And so it went on: the cobbler's wife was found to have a little bag of barley, and a widow who lived at the other end of the village some dried herbs, and on and on until at last the tinker held up a hand and declared the soup ready.

'Fit for an emperor!' he cried.

The soup was carried in state through the village to the Sun and shared out between all the villagers. The miller's wife found some day-old bread and they shared that as well. All who were there declared it the best soup they'd ever eaten and the best party they'd had in a long time.

The tinker just smiled to himself as he quietly ate his share. The next morning, he hefted his pack on his back and headed off to Coate, the stone safely stored away. But the villagers of Liddington never forgot how to make stone soup, and they found that in times of trouble any stone would do.

'Stone Soup' is a very well-known folk tale that occurs across Europe from Russia to Portugal. In Villages of the White Horse, Alfred Williams says that the people of Liddington were very good at making it. Devil's toenails (a kind of oyster), shepherd's crowns (sea urchins) and snake stones (ammonites) are all fossils commonly found alongside flint in the chalky soil of most of Wiltshire.

5

THE ODSTOCK
CURSE

In the old days, the children of the village of Odstock used to play
with the Gypsy children when the Gypsies passed through. The
Gypsies would pile into the church on Sunday, and afterwards
the children would all troop off to Joshua's camp to listen to Old
Mother Lee tell them stories in exchange for a barley bannock or a
few potatoes. But by 1805 that had all changed, and the children
of the village were afraid to even look Mother Lee in the eye.

There were two Gypsy families in the area, the Lees, led by
Mother Lee and her old man Joseph, and the Scamps, led by old
Joshua. Now, at that time, Joshua's eldest daughter, Mary, and
Mother Lee's son, Noah, started walking out together. When they
were married at the end of the harvest, it was in Odstock that
the ceremony was held. Many of the villagers were invited: the
blacksmith, the carpenter and even the church sexton, Hackett.
The Yew Tree Inn supplied the beer, and a fine time was had by all.
The happy young couple went off to a new tent at the encampment
by the chalk pit.

It was a fine wedding, but perhaps it wasn't the best match for
young Mary. Noah was a charmer, and he'd certainly charmed
Mary, but he'd already been in trouble with the law for poaching.

That was normal enough, but it was when he started stealing from his own that the trouble really started. About five months after the wedding, Mother Lee missed some of the tinware that she used to sell in the villages. The old woman was furious. She put about that she'd cursed the thief, then stormed off to the blacksmith to borrow a mirror. When the blacksmith handed over his wife's looking glass he asked her, 'What you are going to do with that?'

'I shall find the thief and my tinware!' cried Mother Lee.

Find it she did. But the answer wasn't what she wanted, for the mirror showed her own son Noah's camp, the tinware sitting as bold as brass in a basket in his tent.

'Perhaps he took it by accident,' Mother Lee said to herself. 'Perhaps he forgot it was mine.'

No mother wants to curse her own son, but it was too late. The curse was already cast.

The next thing to go missing was Joshua Scamp's best coat. It was a fine thing, green velveteen with a yellow collar and brass buttons, and Joshua was proud of it. Like Mother Lee, he was furious when he found it gone, but he wasn't the cursing sort – that was women's business. Instead, he put the word around that the miscreant would come to a different sort of harm if the coat wasn't handed back. Joshua had his own suspicions, and fights started to break out among the Gypsies, but the coat couldn't be found anywhere.

One day, when Joshua and his younger daughter Nellie were at the blacksmith's, the girl getting her donkey re-shod and her father his knives sharpened, the girl happened to look out at the road. What she saw made her jaw drop.

'Dad!' she cried. 'See that that man there? He's wearing your coat!'

Joshua looked up pretty smartish at that. Walking along the road was a tinker with a pack overflowing with bootlaces and rabbit skins. He was resplendent in green velveteen.

'Hoy!' called out Joshua. 'Where'd you get that coat?'

The tinker stopped and stared. 'I got it off a man in Salisbury.'

Joshua started to shake his head.

The tinker's eyes flashed with offence. 'If you don't believe me, come with me and I'll take you to him.'

Joshua had a pretty clear idea who'd taken the coat, so he and Nellie went to Salisbury with the tinker. But when they arrived, there was no one to meet. Joshua had been tricked. The tinker wasn't a tinker at all; he was an undercover police officer. As soon as they arrived in the city, Joshua was arrested for the theft of a valuable cart horse at South Newton.

Joshua's friends and relations immediately came forward and swore that he'd been at the camp with them the night of the theft. It should have been enough to get him off, but who trusted the word of a Gypsy? Certainly not the magistrates at Salisbury. Joshua Scamp was convicted and sentenced to be hanged.

Joshua went to his end with dignity, but it must have taken the good folks of Salisbury many years to forget the day he was killed. Everything was done with due ceremony. Joshua was shown his coffin, made by the very same Odstock carpenter who'd danced at his daughter's wedding, and he pronounced it good. There were cheers and screams as he was led to the scaffold, the hood already over his head.

'Any last wishes?' asked the hangman.

'I should like,' said Joshua in a calm voice, 'to see my friends one last time.'

The hood was pulled from his head and Joshua looked down at his friends and family in the front row. His two daughters and his son were there. But not his son-in-law. His gaze lingered on his eldest daughter a moment longer than the rest.

After the deed was done, there was fighting all the way down Fisherton Street to the Market Square. The inns quietly closed up and bolted their doors. Hundreds came to the funeral at Odstock, Gypsies and villagers alike, and Joshua was laid to rest on the south side of the churchyard.

The horse-stealing didn't stop. If anything, it got worse. The thief took a fine chestnut hunter, a lord's horse. It was an unusual beast with a long silver mane and tail. Hard to steal, harder to hide, even harder to sell. Too hard. Was it just that the police caught up with him? Or was it his mother's curse as well? Whatever the reason, carelessness or fate, Noah Lee's luck had run out. He was sentenced and he was hanged.

Folks didn't turn out for him as they had for his father-in-law. As soon as he was dead his young widow, with her baby in her arms, went to her own family and the Lees and she told them this: 'I went to my father in jail, and as soon as he saw me he took my hand and he said, "Now, Mary, you listen to me. I'll not blame you if you know, but like as not it's your man stole that cart horse." I swore that I didn't know, but once he said it, I was sure he was right. I was set to go the magistrate and tell 'em everything, but my old dad he went on, "Now, Mary, I'm seventy-one years old, and I've had a good life – longer than I thought it would be – and your man's not yet twenty-one, and there's you with your babe on the way. Noah could have a long life too, if he plays it careful, and you tell him that. You're not to breathe a word of this to the law. Let me go off and meet my maker, while your young man makes his way through life." If he'd not said that, I'd have gone straight to them, and my dad would be here right now. But you can't disobey your old dad, now, can you?'

After that, a kind of cult grew up around Joshua's grave. Everyone was very kind to Mary and her baby, and saw that she didn't go hungry, but no one grieved that much when Noah Lee's small son died. But it was the grave that drew people. Not just the Scamps and the Lees. Other Gypsy families passing through would lay a card or a bunch of flowers on the grave, and on the first anniversary of Joshua's death, a scant few weeks after Noah was hanged, a party was held there by the grave.

The Church and its staff put up with it for a while. Everyone sympathised with the family and the sad story that Mary had told, but after a few years Joshua started to fade from the villagers' minds as new stories took his place.

But he hadn't faded for the Gypsies.

They turned up as usual on the anniversary of his death, and Mother and Joseph Lee led the festivities as they always did. After availing themselves of the stocks of beer and cider that Bracher at the Yew Tree had got in, everyone set to improving the grave. Flowers were planted all over it and at the foot they put a young yew tree.

Yews live long, long lives but they are quick growers. The sapling was soon an unsightly and straggly tree – at least in the eyes of Hackett the sexton. He marched to the Gypsy camp and told them to pull it down. He was sent packing with jeers and laughter. The Gypsies would never pull down Joshua's tree. Never.

So, one night, Hackett got together with Revd Groves and Hodding the churchwarden and they grubbed out the tree. The Gypsies soon heard. But the first the villagers knew of it was the next Sunday morning, when a procession of Gypsies came through the village with Mother Lee at their head. Into the church they went, and they smashed up everything they could lay their hands on. The pews were broken and hurled through the windows. The altar table was kicked over and the cross left broken on the floor. Hassocks were split and strewn across the nave. Then they raced out to the churchyard and cut down all the other yews. They even cut the bell rope. When there was nothing left to destroy, they ran through the village, shouting and yelling, towards the pub. Bracher was wise. He opened the doors and let them in. They ate and drank until there was nothing left.

Only old Mother and Joseph Lee stayed behind at the church. With great solemnity, Mother Lee removed her bonnet and pressed it into her husband's hands. Then she placed a hand over her eyes and began to curse.

To the Vicar she said, 'You'll not be preaching this time next year.'

To Hodding the churchwarden she cried, 'No son of yours will ever farm your land.'

And to Sexton Hackett, 'You shall be dead before a twelve-month is out.'

Then, full of dignity, the two of them walked back to their camp.

But it didn't end there. Next morning, Mother Lee found her shawl was missing and realised she must have dropped it in the church. Without another thought, she set off to retrieve it. In the night, though, the villagers had been busy. They had recruited a whole team of special constables to guard the church. They wouldn't let Mother Lee inside. They shoved her away when she tried to get past them, then they locked the church door against her. When she heard the key click in the lock, Mother Lee's fury rose to boiling point.

She spun around, pointed at the door and cried, 'Any person who hereafter locks this door will die before a year is out.'

The Gypsies left the village pretty sharpish after that. Before they left, Mother Lee placed a bunch of flowers on Joshua's grave, and told the blacksmith, 'Before I return, my wishes will come true.'

The Vicar was the first. Soon after the Gypsies went, he got a sore throat that wouldn't shift. Soon, you could hardly understand a word he said, and he had to give up preaching. It wasn't long before he died. People started muttering about the curse.

For Hodding, the churchwarden, the curse began to bite when his dairy herd caught anthrax. All had to be slaughtered and

buried. The following spring his lambs all died, and that year his wife had miscarriage after miscarriage. Hodding knew what he had to do to save himself and his wife. He knew that he had to leave the land that his family had worked for centuries. In desperation, he and his wife packed up their bags and emigrated to Australia.

Then it was Hackett's turn. One day he didn't show up for work, and when the villagers went out searching they found his body lying by the side of the road without a mark on it.

Nobody dared lock the church door. It stayed unlocked till 1900. A carpenter, not from the village, had been brought in to fix the church gate. In the Yew Tree that night he laughed when he was told the story.

'You superstitious fools!' he cried. 'I'll lock that door, and then you'll see.'

Everyone told him not to, but he was determined. The whole village turned up to watch. The bolt was so rusted it was hard to throw across and he struggled to turn the key but, at last and with a great flourish, it was done.

'Well,' said the sexton, 'only so many months until Christmas and the end of the year...' The carpenter laughed, but the villagers noted that the sexton was not smiling.

For some months it looked as if the carpenter had got away with it, but then he was found ill in bed, clutching his stomach. He was packed off to hospital in Salisbury, but they could do nothing for him there, and sent him to the bigger hospital at Bournemouth.

After a week or so of treatment he was feeling much better. One night when dinner arrived he even felt up to joking. 'I shall get so fat in here that my people will not know me when I get home.' They say he was dead before he finished his meal.

The church remained unlocked until the 1930s. When the Vicar was taken so sick that he had to go away to convalesce, a locum was brought in. Perhaps no one told him the story, or perhaps he too thought it was superstitious nonsense, but he went and locked the church. He too was dead within the year. When the Vicar returned, he threw the key in the Ebble.

And there it might have ended, but the curse would take one more victim. In 1990, nearly 200 years after it all began, a young man who'd heard the story took it upon himself to find the key. He worked out where he thought the Vicar had thrown the key, calculated how much it might have moved with the flowing of the river, then took a few days off work to search through the mud to find it.

On the way home from the river the first night, he was knocked off his motorbike and killed. No one knows if he found the key, but for another seventeen years no one attempted to lock the door.

But it's a sad fact that it's hard, in this day and age, to leave a church open all day and all night, and after 200 years it was decided that enough was enough. In 2007 the Bishop of Salisbury and the current Gypsy Queen met at Odstock and she lifted the curse. For the first time since the curse was laid down, the people of Odstock can now rest easy knowing that they and their church are safe and sound.

> *This is a true story. An account of the original events was written by Hiram Witt in the 1870s, describing what he remembered happening as a boy. I am indebted to John Chandler for providing Witt's account in his* Wiltshire Folklore and Legends.

6

THE BARROW
THIEVES

Everyone knew there was gold in the mounds up on Bowerchalke
Down. In the valleys below, farmers had for years been turning up
bits of gold: little badges with coats of arms, broken rings and odd
coins with leaping horses on them. But that was nothing. It was
the mounds that held the serious loot. There had always been hill-
diggers, burrowing into the barrows and emerging triumphant,
they said, with whole suits of armour and bulky rings prised from
skeletal hands, but hardly anyone had gone out digging for years.

The rumour was that the old men of the village, when they were
young men, had gone up the hill with their spades and shovels and
started to dig. It wasn't long, it was said, before the dull sheen of
gold was seen through the dirt, and a heavy golden table exposed.
The men were astonished at their luck – so astonished that one of
them cried out, 'There it is!' Immediately, the table sank out of
sight and no matter how far they scrabbled down through the dirt,
it could not be found.

Adam Thick and James Barter had other ideas. So what if their
grandfathers had failed? They were just stupid old men. James,
and especially Adam, knew better. They got together another five
young men from the village with whom to share their plans.

'You got to have seven,' said Adam. 'It's lucky, see?'

In the back room of the pub, the seven heads bent together and six of them listened to Adam. 'We're not daft like them old men,' said Adam.

'I've been doing research, and this is how it's going to go. First, we'll learn a lesson from them dafties: you've got to be silent all the while you're digging. Not a word until the thing is out of the earth! Got that?'

The young men all nodded, and supped their beer.

'Next, we can only get it out between the first and the second strikes of midnight – and before you say that's impossible, I've got a plan.' He tapped the side of his nose. 'And not only that, I tell you that we can't even breathe when we're hauling out the loot. You've got to hold your breath, the lot of you.'

He told them James had found a place where they could stash the gold and cut it up if they were lucky enough to find any. Then he got them to swear a solemn oath to keep it a secret on pain of death. They all swore the oath, and each man went away that night dreaming his own private dreams of fortune.

They waited till it was a full moon. Adam had said they had to go up there without torches, as torches would surely be seen from the village below. He'd selected the mound, he said, when he was up there with the sheep. They took the long, boggy path across the meadows. When they reached the bottom of the hill, they crept up the side to the chosen barrow and began to dig.

They dug and they dug, the earth piling up around them, their breath condensing in the cold night air until at last a spade clanked against something hard. Something metal. Using their hands now, they brushed away the earth, and there, gleaming in the moonlight, was a thick sheet of gold. They all stopped to stare at it, but none of them breathed a word. Then, as quickly as they could, they uncovered the whole thing. It was a coffin made of solid gold. The excitement crackled through the silent men as they secured the ropes underneath and tied them firmly on top.

Their breath puffed out clouds of white in the cold air as they waited. They heard the bell of Bower Chalke church ring half past

eleven, and they waited. They heard it ring the quarter hour, and they waited.

Then, as the bell began to ring the midnight hour, they sucked in their breath and with their chests bursting with the need to breathe they heaved and they hauled until the coffin was lying on the grass beside them. For a moment they paused and stared down at their prize, then, one by one, they placed the ropes over their shoulders and began to haul the coffin away across the Downs. Still none of them spoke a word, but their breath no longer puffed white in the cold night air.

They didn't come home that night. In the morning their wives and mothers raised the alarm and a gang of old men went out to search the Downs. It wasn't long before they found the barrow, naked and empty to the sky. The old men shook their heads and went back down the hill. They went to the wives and mothers with their caps in hand and told them that they'd never see their young men again.

After that, no one touched the mounds. It wasn't until the archaeologists came and began to excavate them in full daylight that anyone thought it wise to go near a barrow again.

But the old men were wrong. It was true that Adam Thick, James Barter and their friends never came down to the village again. But they were seen. When the moon is full and the sky is clear and crisp on a winter's night, you can see them still. Seven men, with ropes over their shoulders, they haul their golden coffin here and there all over Bowerchalke Down, searching all night for the coffin's true resting place. Yet they will never find it, even if they go right over the barrow. They will pull that coffin over the Downs forever, and they will never speak, nor will you see their breath condense white in the chill night air.

> *There were barrow thieves all over the Downs – hill-diggers searching for treasure, whether from ancient graves or more recent abandoned hoards. The episode of the sinking table is actually located at Wick Farm near Marlborough. I moved it to Bowerchalke where the ghostly thieves can be seen, but the rules that Adam Thick imposed on his friends were common knowledge across the Downs.*

7

THE DEVIL IN WILTSHIRE

The Devil's been around in Wiltshire longer than anywhere else. Not surprising really when you think about it, considering how much religion there's always been in the county. When they built Avebury, the Devil started to get nervous, but it's when they began building Stonehenge that he got himself in real high dudgeon.

'There's far too much religion in Wiltshire!' he cried, and set off to do something about it. He went up onto the Plain and started to dig up the earth with his shoulder-bone shovel. This shovel was enormous – you'd not want to meet the cow it came from on a dark night – so he soon had enough for his purpose. He scooped up the huge pile of earth in the shovel and set it on his shoulder. Then he set off towards Avebury to bury the stones.

The priests and priestesses there soon realised he was coming. They began on their chants and incussations so that when the Devil arrived he couldn't get in. He walked all around the Henge, all the way up the avenue, right up close to the Sanctuary, past the long barrow at West Kennet where the red-eared dog waits, all the way down to the barrow at Beckhampton, along the Avenue there and back up to the Henge again, but still he couldn't get in.

The priests and priestesses chanted as if their lives depended on it. The Devil longed to cover his ears to shut out the sound, but to do that he would have to put the shovel down. He was wise to them, alright. Round he went again, but by now the shovelful of earth was getting pretty heavy, and by the time he got up to West Kennet he was pretty fed up, but he set out towards Beckhampton nonetheless. The shovel was so heavy, though, that by the time he'd walked a few paces he'd had enough, and he dropped the earth where he stood.

And that's Silbury Hill.

But the Devil never learns. Like the old dog he is, all he knows are the old tricks.

Many, many years later in mortal time, but the blink of an eye to the Devil, Marlborough and Devizes were quarrelling. I don't know what the quarrel was about, and by that time neither did they. Was it about who had the best market? About the prettiness of the girls? Who knows? But it hardly mattered anymore, such was the fury between the towns.

In Marlborough they grew so angry that they decided to take direct action, and they called the Devil.

'Destroy Devizes!' they said.

Now, the Devil was only too happy to comply, but he only had room for one idea in his head. So he took his shovel, a metal one now but just as big, and he went back to Salisbury Plain. He scooped up a huge shovelful of earth and set off to smother Devizes.

When the people of Devizes heard he was coming, they were terrified. They all gathered in the Market Place in a great panic.

The Vicar of St Mary's cried, 'We must pray to God that he will deliver us!'

Everyone fell to their knees and prayed. Their prayers were so strong that St John, who was visiting Salisbury at the time, heard them. He came rushing to Devizes to find out what was wrong.

'The Devil is coming to destroy us!' the people cried.

St John knew the Devil of old, so he listened, and he thought, and soon enough he said, 'I think I have a plan. This is what we'll do...'

Now, it was a foggy night and, not to put too fine a point on it, the Devil was lost. He could hardly see his hand in front of his face, and the shovelful of earth was once again getting heavy. So he was relieved when he bumped into an old man with grey hair and a white beard, who was walking steadily along the road.

'Is this the way to Devizes?' asked the Devil.

The man stared at him a moment, then laughed. 'If you could tell me, I'd be that grateful! I set off from Marlborough for Devizes, ooh, I don't know when – but I can tell you this, my hair was black in them days!'

When the Devil heard this he was horrified, and he ditched his load then and there.

And that's how Cley Hill was formed.

By now it was nearly midnight, and there is only one place in Wiltshire where the Devil can be at midnight: in his own den at Clatford Bottom. His den was a peaceful place, away from the fires and torments of Hell, but the thing was, many years ago, somebody had blocked his way in with a great stone. It was a long time since the Devil had been able to snuggle up by his own fire. So, as he did every night, the Devil conjured up a team of four white oxen and yoked them up to the great capstone and set them to heaving, and he set himself at the front end of the team and heaved as well. The Devil's an optimist, and he thought: 'Maybe this time it'll work.' His little white, red-eared dog roused itself from beside the fire below and came up to have a look. But it was no good; the stone wouldn't budge, the sweat was popping from the Devil's brow and by half past midnight he had such a thirst on him that he'd have done anything for a drink.

Now, the only way the Devil can have a drink is if someone raises a toast in his honour. So he put his ear to the ground and he listened. Time passed and time passed, until the time of the Civil War, and at last he heard something that made his ears prick up.

In the Catherine Wheel in Salisbury, a group of young Cavaliers sat at their cups. One of them raised his glass and cried, 'To the King!'

'To King Charles!' they all chorused back.

'To Prince Rupert!' cried another, and they all drank to their commander.

'To my wife, Jane,' murmured one, and the others laughed but raised their glasses.

'To my betrothed, Lacy!' cried another.

'To Moll, who stands on the corner at Carfax, back in Oxford!' cried one, and they all toasted that.

When they had been through all the women they had ever known, and quite a few they hadn't, they were at a loss.

'We can't drink without a toast,' slurred one, 'and the landlord will insist on keeping the drinks coming.'

'There is one we haven't toasted yet,' said another, twirling his long moustache. 'The Devil!'

The Devil grinned, and he listened hard. But everyone burst out laughing.

'We can't toast him,' they cried. 'He doesn't exist! We can't toast something that doesn't exist!'

The Devil fumed, but at least there was something he could do.

The first that the soldiers in the Catherine Wheel knew about it was the cloud of blue smoke spreading through the inn. Then the Devil appeared, all flashing eyes, cloven hooves, horns and whipping red tail. He grabbed the man who had proposed the toast to him by the scruff of the neck, and dragged him off down to Hell.

That was satisfying, but he was still thirsty. So he put his ear to the ground again and he listened. Time passed and time passed.

There's no one as thirsty as a navvy, they say, but that night it wasn't the navvy who'd been out drinking. Building the railway at Newton Tony was thirsty work, but it was tiring too, and the navvy had gone back to his lodgings for an early night. The problem was his landlady only had two rooms, and of course one was her own. The other belonged to her son, Tom, who could drink a navvy under the table, or at least was willing to try. The navvy shared his room.

The navvy slept soundly until he heard young Tom staggering up the stairs and stumbling into bed. But no sooner was he in bed than he fell straight out again. The navvy groaned, and pulled his pillow over his head. Tom crawled back into bed, but yet again he fell out. And then again. Then the navvy heard him get up and shamble down the stairs. He heard the back door open, then the sound of the pump, and then Tom coming back up the stairs.

The navvy watched as Tom came into the room with a glass of water. Very sensible, thought the navvy, but Tom didn't drink it. Instead, with exaggerated care, he placed it under his bed.

'What are you doing?' cried the navvy, unable to keep his peace any longer.

'Why,' said Tom, as if it was obvious, 'the Devil 'e's in my bed, and 'e's jealous 'cos I've 'ad a drink, and 'e 'asn't. So I reckoned that, if I got 'im a drink, 'e'd be happy and leave me to sleep in peace.'

And hearing that, the Devil shot straight out of the bed, grabbed the glass, bolted straight out of the door and onto the Plain beyond. He drank the glass down in one gulp.

'Water!' he cried in horror.

And the Devil was so displeased that he shot straight back to Hell and wasn't seen in Wiltshire again. At least not on that night.

The Devil gets everywhere, but his favourite trick in Britain is creating landscape by accident. Huge numbers of hills around the country were created by the Devil getting fed up with carrying heavy shovelfuls of earth around. It is very common in cultures that have kept alive the oral tradition to explain landscape features in stories. The songlines of the Australian Aborigines are perhaps the best known, but stories of this kind stretch from the Americas to Japan. Are the Devil stories of Britain a folk memory of our own creation myths, the Devil taking the place of the old gods and heroes?

8

LADY DIANA
SPENCER

It was a very casual way to start a marriage. A throwaway line at a party at Vauxhall Gardens. The company was bright, and laughter rang out as the ladies teased the sole gentleman of the party, and tapped him with their fans.

'Why, Bully, you must marry! You must admit you will soon be past your best!' cried Miss Egerton, blushing at her boldness.

Bully wasn't interested in her, but he listened. Laughing, he turned to the lady next to him and said, 'Will you have me?'

Lady Diana Spencer looked the 3rd Viscount St John up and down.

'Yes,' she said, 'to be sure.'

Her chaperone, the Duchess of Bedford, heaved a sigh of relief at the girl's cool acceptance. Lady Diana, 'Di' to her friends, was already twenty-one. There had been a number of unsuitable suitors. As long as those casual words could be made into reality, this was progress indeed.

Frederick St John, Lord Bolingbroke, otherwise known as 'Bully', wasn't the best catch for the great-granddaughter of Sarah Churchill, the Duchess of Marlborough. A mere viscount with a simple Wiltshire estate could not compare with the wealth Sarah and her husband had amassed in the late seventeenth century. But that was fifty years ago, and the family's fortunes had changed. Bully's estates at Lydiard Tregoze and Battersea were respectable and, if the man was a bully by nature as well as by name, what did it matter? In the 1750s the wife of a lord was there for one thing and one thing alone: to bear sons to continue the family name. Bully was also handsome and wild. Di was keen.

His friends persuaded him that Lady Di was a good catch. She was witty and good-looking, a talented artist, and sure to bring a handsome dowry.

They were married. Lady Di soon discovered that although his estate at Lydiard Tregoze was pleasant, Bully didn't have much money. She found too that as his wife she ranked beneath his main interests: horseracing, gambling and other women. Bully was not discreet. His current paramour was Maria Coventry, the wife of Lord Coventry. Maria also had another lover: the King's younger brother. She was amusing, but for Bully one good reason for marrying Lady Di had been to nullify the risk he'd have to marry Maria if her elderly husband died or divorced her. A mistress does not make a good wife, especially if she's already two-timing you with someone else. As for the racing and the gambling, such things were perfectly acceptable for a young bachelor, but Bully didn't realise they were less suitable for a married man with responsibilities.

Meanwhile, Di didn't immediately fulfil her end of the bargain. It took a tense three years before she gave birth to a son, George; an heir to the Bolingbroke estate. After that, things seemed better between Di and Bully. He was still haemorrhaging money, but Di found herself a job as a Lady of the Bedchamber to Queen Charlotte, George III's young bride. She secured Bully a position as a Gentleman of the Bedchamber to the King.

Being a Lady of the Bedchamber was not as glamorous as it might seem. It involved a lot of tedious standing around, and the ladies were forbidden food and drink during the long hours of duty. It was particularly hard on Di when she was pregnant with her second child. The job and the continuing money woes took their toll: the child died aged only five months.

Despite their troubles, everyone said that Lord and Lady B. rubbed along tolerably well together over the next few years, and indeed, a third child, Frederick, a spare to go with the heir, was born in 1763. But with duty fulfilled, Bully simply ignored his wife and Lady Di became restless. Bully's affairs had never stopped. While Di was posing for a portrait by Joshua Reynolds, she didn't know that the famous portraitist had just completed a portrait of Bully's present mistress, Nelly O'Brien. When commissioning the portrait of his wife, Bully said to Reynolds, 'You must give the eyes something of Nelly or it will not do.'

The marriage cracked. Lady Di realised that her dreams would never come true with Bully. Life with him had become intolerable. She refused to be mired in Wiltshire forever, so she packed her bags and left her home, her husband and her two young sons. But there was another reason to leave. Lady Di had found another man. But while it was acceptable – just – for Bully to have mistresses, a wife taking a lover was not accepted at all.

'There were mud stains on the sofa,' said William Flockton, her footman.

'Not just that,' said Elizabeth Thomas, her maidservant. 'The pillows were on the floor and covered in hair powder! And they were in the room together with the curtains drawn in the middle of the day.'

'And this happened every day,' added Flockton.

In those days, divorce was shocking and meant ruin for the woman. Lady Di and Bully were not divorced, just separated. It wasn't amicable. If they happened to meet, they completely ignored each other. She rented a house in Mayfair. There she started to meet her new man in earnest.

Topham Beauclerk had royal blood in his veins. He was the grandson of a love child of Charles II and his beloved orange-seller Nell Gwynn, and it was Nellie's temperament that ran true through the family's veins. Topham's own father was described as 'Nell in person, with the sex altered'.

Topham was tall, dark and handsome like his great-grandfather the King. He was fashionable, clever and witty, he collected rare

books, and he was an intimate of
one of the great minds of the day,
Samuel Johnson. The two men were
always together, Beauclerk tempting
Johnson to mischief: annoying the
market traders of Covent Garden,
rowing on the Thames, mucking
about in churchyards. In short,
Topham was one of the most
agreeable men who could
possibly exist – if he was
in the right company and
in a good humour.

It was easy enough for
Topham and Lady Di to meet,
as they moved in the same circles, but how to get to know each
other better? Topham became a frequent visitor at Lady Di's house
in Mayfair. But it wasn't until a visit to Tunbridge Wells that
things started to get serious. With servants watching everywhere,
families moving freely through the interconnecting rooms, and
cumbersome clothing to negotiate, an affair needed careful
planning. But at least a spa was more discreet than being in town.

Pleading a headache, Lady Di begged leave to stay in the house
one morning when her family went out to enjoy the pursuits of
the spa. She waited, and soon enough, Topham arrived. Lady Di
rang for a servant. When Flockton appeared, she asked for a glass
of water. Flockton stayed while she drank, his eyes flicking from
her ladyship to the young man. When Flockton took the empty
glass, he didn't go back to the kitchen but lurked in the shadows
of the hall.

After a while, the footman was rewarded. The door opened,
and Lady Di and Topham crept out. They made their way into the
back parlour in which a ladies' couch had recently been installed.
Flockton pressed his ear to the door and he grinned as he listened.

The deed only took ten minutes, but the die was cast. When
they returned to London Topham visited all the time. It was soon

noticed among the maidservants that Lady Di's stays wouldn't lace as tight as usual. Some things can't be hidden. The servant's loose tongues soon had the neighbourhood watching Lady Di's every move. Flockton and Elizabeth Thomas were dismissed for gossiping. The child was born in utmost secrecy and spirited away to a wet nurse. But despite the desperate secrecy, the news was out and Bully had to act.

Divorce proceedings began, and the servants were hauled up to tell their tales. Flockton and Thomas had plenty to say about their mistress. Soon the story was well known to all. But despite having her name dragged through the dirt, Lady Di was released from her marriage to marry Topham and recover her young daughter. The marriage was happy at first, and Di was free to pursue her other love: art.

But Lady Di didn't get a simple happy ending. Bully's excesses caught up with him. He developed a palsy of the brain and was soon raving mad. He had to be committed to a lunatic asylum. Many blamed Lady Di for this but, though he had mourned her loss with apparent sincerity, he had not mended his ways. His womanising may well have caused his illness. Topham, too, soon became ill. The illness made him an unpleasant husband to Lady Di, and he was rude and unpleasant to all of his friends. It could only have been with relief that she greeted his death in 1780. She didn't take a third husband.

Bully's death in 1787 meant that Lady Di was at last reunited with her two sons from her first marriage, and able to introduce them to the two daughters and son she'd had with Topham. She must have hoped that all would now be well in her life. Sadly, her story would have a tragic epilogue that no one could have foreseen.

Mary, her eldest daughter, aged only sixteen, went to stay with her half-brother George and his wife at Lydiard. The brother and sister conceived a passion for each other. Worse, they conceived a child. The birth was hushed up, but another child soon followed, and the lovers fled to the Continent with their sons. In the end the relationship fell apart and George crept back to his wife. Mary managed to find a husband abroad, but Di's heart was broken.

She must have felt punished indeed for her own youthful actions. In the end, though, she was rewarded. Mary had many children with her husband. The eldest was given into Lady Di's care. Di's last years were perhaps her happiest, looking after her granddaughter and making a living from the art she loved so much.

Lady Di's life has echoes of that of her distant relation Diana, Princess of Wales. In the eighteenth century, however, divorce was extremely damaging to a woman's reputation and meant that a mother lost all contact with her children. The expectation was that a separated or divorced woman would live a quiet, frugal life with no society. Diana was lucky to have her art to support herself. In Lydiard House you can visit the Blue Closet and see many of her drawings and Wedgwood china decorated with her designs.

9

THE GHOSTLY HUNT

Squire Parker of Lushill loved hunting more than anything else in the world. He lived for the hunt and would have spent every day out riding with the hounds if he could. Nothing gave him more pleasure than to ride with his retainers and friends down the hill and through his park in pursuit of his own fat deer.

One balmy June evening, while out hunting in the long summer light, he went further than usual. Alone, he strayed beyond his own lands into the woodland near Nun Eaton. He moved slowly among the trees until he came to a clearing. Immediately, he stilled his horse with a jerk of the reins, for there in front of him stood a white stag. It was white from the tips of its ears to its gleaming white hooves. Its antlers, all seven tines of them, were pure white. Only its eyes were dark, and made darker by the whiteness of the rest. Parker caught his breath in wonder.

For a moment, the animal seemed unaware of his presence and simply stood alert and still. Then it lifted its head and sniffed the air. As soon as it sensed him it plunged off into the undergrowth. Parker gave chase, thrashing his horse through the trees, but the stag was fast and Parker didn't know these woods well. He soon lost it in the gathering gloom and went home empty-handed.

That night he dreamed of the white stag. As soon as he awoke the next morning he told his friends what he had seen and together they rode off in search of the stag. All held their breath as they rode to the clearing, none really believing they would see the creature, but all hoping they would. But there, standing silent in the dappled sunlight, stood the white stag. They gave chase, but again it soon lost them among the trees and no matter how much they searched they could not find it.

The next day, Parker gathered his friends together and again they rode into the wood, and again the stag bolted when they approached and again they lost it among the trees. And so it was the next day, and the next, and the day after that. Parker was obsessed and could think of nothing else save the stag. He hardly ate, and his clothes began to hang loose on him. Dark hollows developed under his eyes and, even though he spent every day hunting, every night he hunted in his dreams. One by one his friends fell away, dismissing him as mad, until he hunted only with his retainers, and even they would not have stayed had not his wife begged them to look after him. People began to say it was just a matter of time until he rode away and didn't come back.

Every day he returned to the same spot in the Nun Eaton woods and every day, without fail, the stag was there. As he arrived, the stag would turn its head towards him, and he would be caught by those dark, solemn eyes as if there was a pact between them. In that moment he wouldn't know who was the hunter and who was the hunted. But the moment would pass, and the stag would dip its antlers and run, and Parker would give chase. He hardly knew what he would do if he did catch it, but catch it he must. But at the end of the day he was always disappointed. His failure preyed on him more and more until one night, as he and his men rode home in the gathering gloom, he stopped dead, stood up in his stirrups and shook his fist at the heavens.

'I swear, to any god that might be listening, that I will not rest until I hold that stag's antlers in my hands!'

Nothing was said of this that night at dinner but in the morning only his most loyal retainers went out to the wood with him. The stag was there and turned its lustrous eyes on Parker and he stared back, daring it to move. It plunged into the wood, and Parker flew after it. All day long he chased it, pounding through the wood, chasing the animal out across the fields and splashing across the ford at the Thames, past Castle Eaton and back again. Never had he held it so long. He felt a wildness take him and he cried aloud with joy.

Throughout the daylight hours his retainers stayed by his side. As the light started to fade, the stag led them back towards the wood again. The trees were shadowy against the evening sky, and as the purple darkness deepened the retainers fell away, spurring their horses home.

Parker hardly noticed. He bent low over his horse's neck and raced on, crashing through the trees, not caring that they tore at his hair and whipped at his face, ripped his clothes and tripped his horse on their roots. He thought of only one thing: catch the white stag!

He found himself back in the clearing, and there stood the stag in the last of the light. In that semi-darkness, the animal seemed to glow and again Parker stopped to marvel at its beauty. For a long moment, hunter and hunted stared at each other, measured each other, equal to equal, until Parker bowed his head, unable to hold the stag's gaze any longer. When he looked up, it was gone.

With a low groan, he spurred his horse into the gloom. Here and there in the darkness he caught a glimpse of a gleaming white flank or glittering hooves, but no matter how hard he pushed his horse, he couldn't gain on the stag.

Then, somewhere behind him, he became aware of the sound of another horse. Thinking it was one of his retainers returned to him, he turned around. Just a few paces behind him stood a horse and rider. The rider wore a wide-brimmed hat low over his face, and in the darkness Parker realised with a shiver that the rider glowed with same light that lit the stag.

For a moment, he came to his senses, and knew that it would be wise to be away, back home, sitting by the fire with his wife at his side. He nearly turned to go. His hand was on the bridle to turn his horse about. But in the woods he glimpsed the stag, and immediately the other rider gave chase. Let this man catch the stag? Without realising what he was doing, Parker urged his horse after the rider. All thoughts of home were gone.

Now, it was different. Always the stag was visible ahead, glinting in the darkness, and when his horse stepped in the hoofprints of the broad-hatted rider then the trees bowed to let him pass and he felt only the tickle of their leaves on his cheek.

The stag led them out of the wood, and they chased it across the ford and over the river. On and on they chased. To Parker it seemed that they wheeled backwards and forwards in the starlight. Past Highworth, its lights gleaming in the darkness, then spinning back and round towards Broad Blunsdon. By now it was so late that only a few lights still shone in the village. The rider veered away, and Parker thought he was heading back yet again to Nun Eaton wood, but then he caught a glimpse of the stag up on Castle Hill.

The going was slower now, the low hill rising up, fringed by trees, the star-spangled sky and, there, the lustrous form of the stag picking its way upwards. Parker followed the rider up after the stag, and by the light of the moon saw white hounds writhing around the horse's legs and, as he drew closer, saw the hounds had fiery eyes and red ears.

The stag stood on the ridgeline, radiant against the dark trees that ran round the top of the hill. The rider approached, the hounds mad to go after the stag. No sound could be heard. Parker followed as if in a dream. Then the rider's horse stepped back and the hounds lay down at his feet. As they watched, the rider gestured for Parker to come forward.

Parker dismounted and stepped up to the stag. It stood quiet, its flanks hardly moving, and watched him approach. He hardly knew what he was going to do, but very gently he reached out and stroked the smooth white hair at its shoulder. The stag's flesh was warm and firm under his hand, and seemed to relax into his strokes. Then, as if compelled, Parker lifted his hands and laid them on the velvet soft antlers.

There was a blinding flash of light. In that moment of brilliance he saw the rider raise his broad hat and reveal that he had but one eye. Then the rider, the hounds and the stag were gone, and for a moment Parker stood alone in the darkness on the top of the hill.

The next thing he knew, he was opening his eyes to see the grey dawn sky above him. He remembered the night before. Just a dream? He rolled onto his side and saw he was in the grounds of his house, back on Lushill. And beside him on the grass lay a pair of velvety white antlers. He caught his breath and reached out to touch them. But as soon as he laid a hand on them, they turned to dust.

This story was collected by Alfred Williams in A Wiltshire Village. *In England the Wild Hunt is led by the old Saxon god Woden, and in Wiltshire Woden is a powerful figure. He built to the Wansdyke – Woden's ditch – that runs the breadth of the county. Woden, or Odin as he is known in Norse mythology, is the leader of the gods and wore a wide-brimmed hat. He had only one eye because he had sacrificed the other at the Spring of Mimir to gain wisdom. The Wild Hunt is an unearthly hunt that rides for all eternity, appearing when England is threatened and taking with it lost and evil souls. In Wiltshire this includes Old Coker of Hill Deverill, who was given the choice to go to Hell or to ride in the hunt. In this story, though, the rider and the stag seem much more benign. The house and woods at Nun Eaton are now known as Water Eaton.*

10

THE RAISING OF THE GIANT'S DANCE

War raged between the British and the Saxons. The Saxons had a strong leader, Hengist. The British had no one. But one day a small boat pulled up near Totnes in Devon, and two young men stepped out. One was Ambrosius Aurelianus; the other was Uther Pendragon. They were the sons of one king and the brothers of another. They were children when they fled Britain but now they were warriors returned to set their country to rights. The Britons flocked to Ambrosius's Red Dragon banner, and begged him to accept the kingship.

'First we end this war,' said Ambrosius. 'Then we can think about crowns.'

And end the war he did. First, they tracked Vortigern down in his tower deep in Snowdonia. They burnt the tower and made an end of the old King in revenge for their brother Constans' death. Then they routed Hengist in battle. The Saxon leader was killed in a grim execution, and the rebellion was over. The British lords swore fealty to Ambrosius, and he was crowned High King of Britain.

The young King's first act was to go to Salisbury Plain to see the mound raised over the men killed on the Night of the Long Knives. It was a bleak day, the cold wind ripping over the long grass. Ambrosius drew his cloak close around his body and stared at the low mound. It was still bare earth, save for a few brave tufts of grass bent flat against the wind.

'We can do better than this,' he said to himself. Then, raising his voice, he cried, 'I will raise a monument here that will bring awe to people long after we are dead. These men, who died for peace, will get a memorial that will last until the end of time.'

Masons and carpenters were summoned to design the great work. But every design they showed to Ambrosius was stale and tired. He despaired of finding an architect who could create the memorial of which he dreamed. His advisors saw his disappointment, but none knew how to help save for one – the Bishop of Caerleon.

'There is someone who could help you,' said the bishop. 'You may have heard of him. Years ago, when just a fatherless boy, he prophesied Vortigern's doom. He raised twin dragons from the earth, one red, one white. They fought together and the red dragon won. He has grown in wisdom since that time and if anyone has an answer to your problem, it is him.'

'Who is he?' asked Ambrosius.

'His name,' said the bishop, 'is Merlin.'

Ambrosius commanded that Merlin be fetched. His men searched the length and breadth of Britain. They searched from Dinas Emrys to Northumberland, but they could not find him. Disheartened, Ambrosius recalled them. Some soldiers, returning from a fruitless search of London happened to pass by the spring of Galabes at Over Wallop, not twenty miles from Salisbury Plain. There sat the enchanter among the dripping ferns, as if he had been waiting for them. He told them to take him to the King.

When he arrived on the Plain, he went straight to the burial mound and stood a long time there. His long hair whipped in the wind as he looked around at the scrubby hills, the valleys cutting away to the north, and the woods encroaching from the hills. Then he turned to Ambrosius and smiled.

'I know what you need,' he said. 'Long ago, before your people and mine landed on the shores of Britain and Ireland, there lived here a race of giants. These giants had powers of which you can only dream. They held off all invaders. But there was one thing they could not defeat: sickness. A plague ravaged the land, and the giants watched their children die. Instead of weeping and cursing the gods, they decided that something must be done. One of their powers was to travel in the twinkling of an eye, and so a delegation took themselves to Egypt, where the heart of all mysteries lies, and begged for aid. They were told that far to the south, where the land was fertile, lay great stone circles dedicated to healing. They went to a great plain, far larger than this one, and there they found them. By their arts they carried one back to Ireland and set it high on the top of Mount Killare in the county of Kildare. To this day, if you are washed in water that has run off those stones you will be cured of all your ills. They call it the "Giant's Dance".'

Merlin's eyes twinkled as he looked at the King. 'I can think of no more fitting monument for this site of betrayal and death than a circle of healing. Come, my King, let us go and fetch it!'

Ambrosius knew that this was what he had been looking for. He despatched his brother, Uther, and 1,500 men to Ireland to steal the stones.

When the King of Ireland heard of their coming, he laughed. 'Surely they have enough stones of their own in Britain?'

He was soon laughing on the other side of his face. Uther's men defeated him in battle and brushed his armies aside to march on Mount Killare and the Giant's Dance.

Despite Merlin's words, the soldiers were not expecting much. Wasn't the King of Ireland right? Didn't they have enough stone circles in Britain? But when they reached the hill and saw the structure on the top they stopped dead in their tracks. This was nothing like the rings of stones that dance across Britain from Maes Howe to the Merry Maidens. The great pillars of the Giant's Dance stood taller than any of them, taller than the tallest man. They stood in pairs, one rough and the other smooth, and on top of each pair rested a stone lintel. Scattered all around the circle, inside and out, lay low blue stones. It was a wonder.

'Now,' said Merlin, 'let's bring it down!'

The engineers Uther had brought hurried up the hill. By means of hawsers and ropes they tried to pull the stones down. But they could not.

Merlin laughed at their failure and then rolled up his sleeves. He lifted his right arm – and the great lintels jumped into the air. He lifted his left – and the great sarsens and the blue stones leapt up and danced beside them. Merlin flung his hands high and as the men watched, he whirled the stones about so that they floated high above the hill, each moving in perfect rhythm with the others around it. Rotating his hands, Merlin danced the stones down the hill and laid them one by one in the waiting boats.

They sailed the ships back with speed across the sea and up the Bristol Channel. With his art, Merlin unloaded the stones onto low barges on the Avon. Up its twisting course they took the stones, across to the Wylye and into the other Avon that comes up from the south.

When they reached Salisbury Plain, Merlin danced the stones across the land in the dark of the night and set them down in a heap by the mound to await the King.

In the morning Ambrosius hurried to see the monument he had stolen. When he saw the pile of stones lying around the mound, he was awed by their size. But the jumbled stones made no sense, and soon he was furious.

'Is this what more British – and Irish – blood was spilled to fetch? A great heap of stones that could have been brought from anywhere?'

Merlin grinned, and raised one finger. 'Wait,' he said. 'Call all your nobles, your bishops and your wise men, and you shall see what you shall see.'

So Ambrosius called all his men to the Plain. Merlin raised his hands and made the stones dance again. He whirled them through the air until the rough pillars stood next to the smooth, and the lintels hovered over the top, and the blue stones danced all around them. Then, one by one, he set them down, each in the same place it had sat on Mount Killare.

Men came from far and wide to see the stones and pay their respects to the dead. King Ambrosius founded a nunnery nearby. But just a few short years later, he died. It was his will that he too should be buried at the Giant's Dance. Uther Pendragon, when his time came, was buried there with careful ceremony by his son, young King Arthur. Everyone expected that it would continue as the royal burial ground, even for King Arthur himself. But Uther was the last, for it is well known that there is no grave for Arthur.

It's said that Merlin was offered a plot at the Giant's Dance, but that he refused. They say he had already chosen a mound for his grave at Marlborough. When the archaeologists dug, they found Marlborough Mount to be as empty as her sister, Silbury Hill. So perhaps the old stories are true and Merlin did not die, but still rests in enchanted sleep, and perhaps it's true that King Arthur too is sleeping, waiting to return. And if Arthur returns, and if he wakes Merlin from his sleep, they will put the land to rights and men and women will live well. Perhaps then Merlin will go to his grave in Marlborough Mount, and Arthur will go to his rightful grave at Stonehenge.

This story comes from Geoffrey of Monmouth. Does the fact that Merlin fetches the stones from Ireland represent an ancient folk memory that the blue stones at least really did come from the west? Many people now think they came from the Preseli Hills in Wales. There really were ancient stone circles in Egypt. They are at least 5,000 years old; older than Stonehenge. The stone circle lies in the desert of Nabta Playa, 100km west of Abu Simbel in the far south of Egypt. When the circle was constructed the area was a fertile plain. This Egyptian stone circle may have had astrological significance. As is often claimed for Stonehenge, it is believed to align to the summer solstice.

Merlin's grave is said to lie in Marlborough Mount in the grounds of Marlborough School. The Mount was once thought to be fairly modern, but recently antler picks have been found there. This may mean that it was a comparable monument to Silbury Hill, which is thought to have been constructed with antler picks and cattle thigh-bone shovels around 4,700 years ago.

11

WILL DARRELL'S CHILD

Mother Barnes wasn't expecting to be woken by a pounding at the door in the middle of that cold and damp November night in 1575. Not that it was unusual for her to be woken in that way. She'd come, over the years, to recognise the frantic knocking of a young man about to become a father for the first time. She had got used to be being dragged at all hours across hills and streams to distant farmsteads, and to meeting the apologetic mother-to-be. This knock wasn't like that. It was peremptory, almost angry; the kind of knock that demands an answer. For a moment she considered burrowing further under her blankets and ignoring it but, with a sigh, she realised that it would only attract interest from her neighbours if she didn't go.

From force of habit, she quickly slung her dress on over her shift, wrapped herself in a cloak, and picked up her bag of instruments. Carrying her rushlight holder nervously, she went to the door and pulled it open. A man stood in the doorway.

'Mother Barnes?'

There was embroidery on his stiffened collar and his cuffs. His linen seemed clean. But his hands were rough. A servant, but from a rich house.

'Your services are required,' the man said. 'Lady Knyvett is brought to bed before her time. Will you come?'

Mother Barnes would never have thought such a great lady as the wife of the High Sheriff of Wiltshire would call on her services, and she'd not even heard that the woman was with child. The man's manner was so abrupt that she considered saying no. But to be at the lying-in of a great lady would do her reputation no harm.

'Very well.'

The messenger's horse was cropping at the straggly autumn grass outside her door. The man mounted the horse and pulled Mother Barnes up behind. They rode over the River Lambourn in the village, then turned south towards Hungerford. For about eight miles they rode, until Mother Barnes found herself out of the country she knew well. Then the man pulled his horse to an abrupt stop.

'Mother Barnes,' he began, 'I fear I have brought you here under false pretences. It is not Lady Knyvett who needs your services. It's your choice, but if you decide to go on, I must blindfold you.'

Mother Barnes saw her chance at fame and fortune disappear. But she knew her duty.

'But there is a babe to be born? I am needed?'

'Good woman,' he said, 'this lady has more need of you this night than any charge you've had, I'll warrant.'

'Very well,' said Mother Barnes. 'If there is a babe, and I am needed, then I will go on.'

The man took out a blindfold and tied it around her eyes. Then they rode again, and Mother Barnes didn't know if they rode east or north, south or west. All she could do was hang on tight to the man's cloak.

The journey seemed endless to her. Mile after mile passed, at least as many as they had already come. But eventually they came to a halt. The man helped her down from the horse and peeled off the blindfold. Mother Barnes looked around. A great house rose up before her. Even in the darkness she got a picture of its peaked roofs and tall chimney stacks. The house lay shrouded in darkness except for one light in an upstairs window. Then the door burst open, and light spilled out. A girl ran down the steps, clutching a fat candle in her hand.

'Is this the midwife?' she cried. On the man's nod, she turned to Mother Barnes. 'You must come, oh, you must come now!'

Together they hurried up the steps and into the hall. It was the first time Mother Barnes had been in such a place, and for a moment she paused to gawp at the high-ceilinged hall hung about with tapestries, but the girl chivvied her up a wide flight of stairs.

She was pushed into a large chamber, then the girl fled. In the middle of the room was a large four-poster bed, hung with finely embroidered bed-cloths, and there, in the middle of the bed, lay a woman. That she was in the final stages of labour was to be expected. What was strange was the mask covering her face. The woman was weeping. Mother Barnes rushed to her side, murmuring that everything would be alright.

'I'll see you and your child well, if God wills it.'

But the woman only cried harder. Mother Barnes felt a prickling at the back of her neck. When she looked around, she saw standing by the fireplace a man dressed in black with a crisp white ruff at his throat. Her first instinct was to order him out, for a birthing

was no place for a man, but the look on his face stopped her words before she could say anything. For a long moment she stared at the man, who looked back her with a closed and level gaze.

The woman cried out in pain. With relief, Mother Barnes turned back to the matter in hand. Soon a baby boy was born, wailing and healthy and strong. But no cloths were laid out to clean and wrap him. Mother Barnes frowned, wrapped him up in her own apron and, hooking him up in her arms, headed for the door to find some. The man barred her way.

'Throw the child in the fire,' he said.

The mother gave a scream and Mother Barnes stepped back in horror, curling her arms tighter around the babe.

'No!' she cried. 'No! Sir, what can you mean? He is a strong, healthy child!'

The man stepped closer, and Mother Barnes recoiled from what she saw in his eyes.

'Throw the child in the fire, or I will do it myself.'

'No! Sir, if you don't want this child, this fine boy – see what a fine boy he is – I will take him. I will raise him as my own, or give him to some poor couple who can't have children. Please! He will never know anything of his birth, I swear!'

But the man reached out to take the child. She tried to stop him, but he was so much stronger than her. He ripped the child from her arms and flung him in the fire.

The mother was screaming, the child shrieked and Mother Barnes leapt forward to try to pull the baby out before he burned, but the man held her back. He stirred the coals with his feet so the fire leapt and crackled. When it was done and nothing was left but ashes, he released her and pushed her back towards the bed.

'See to her, and then you will be paid,' he said, and swept out of the room, slamming the door behind him. The mother could not be calmed, but a dose of poppy eventually sent her to sleep. Mother Barnes sat on the bed, unable to believe what had just happened. A piece of the bed-hanging was loose next to her. An idea formed in her mind and she took out her shears and snipped a piece off. Then she went downstairs again.

At the bottom, the man who'd brought her was waiting. His face was grim and white as he silently handed her a bag of gold. She stared at the bag for a long time, but then took it in her hand.

'Come,' said the man. His voice was a rasp of grief. 'Let me take you home. I'm sorry, you will have to wear the blindfold again.'

Mother Barnes thought, 'That is the least thing for you to be sorry about.' But she said nothing, just mounted up on the horse and allowed the blindfold to be tied.

It was late afternoon when she got home and the light was fading as she went inside. Wearily, she sat down at her table, opened her bag of tools and pulled out the piece of embroidered bed-hanging.

'Little child, you will have justice for the crimes against you, for the ending of your life before it was begun. I swear it.'

The very next morning Mother Barnes went to the magistrate at Hungerford and told her tale. The magistrate raised the alarm, and the great houses of the neighbourhood were searched. No one was very surprised when the piece of bed-hanging matched a bed in Littlecote House, just over the border in Wiltshire.

Littlecote was owned by Will Darrell. They called him 'Wild Will', and his bad deeds were the talk of the area. He had been barred from inheriting Littlecote when he father died, the house being left to the old man's mistress. Darrell got it back and after that triumph he took anything that he wanted for his own. No one was surprised at the tale, and no one was surprised when he was put on trial for the murder of the child.

The rumour ran that the mother of the child was his own sister Rachel. She hadn't been seen at Littlecote for some months, people said. Everyone expected that Darrell would be hanged. But it was not to be. The judge at the trial was Sir John Popham, Darrell's cousin, and he was acquitted. The rumour was that he and Popham had come to a deal, and that Popham would inherit Littlecote.

The years passed, five, ten, near on fifteen years, and if anything Darrell's behaviour got worse. Nothing more was said of the murdered child. New atrocities had taken the place of that deed. Darrell seemed untouchable, but people hoped that one day he would get his comeuppance.

Then, one day in 1589, he was found dead by a stile near his home. The story was told that as he was out riding there was a flash of bright light. His horse shied and he fell, but before he hit the ground he saw in the light the figure of a tiny babe reaching out to him.

The Pophams inherited the estate, just as rumour had said all those years before. They held it for many years. The story of Wild Will faded into a story to scare children.

But one night in 1861, the heir to the estate, Francis Popham, not yet six months old and alone in the house with his nursemaid, lay ill at Littlecote. The frightened woman sent for the parents. All night she sat up by the sick baby, listening out in case they returned.

Around midnight, she heard the clank of the gates being flung open, the clatter of horses' hooves on the drive and the screech of the wheels of a carriage as it ground to a halt outside the entrance. The nursemaid heaved a sigh of relief and waited for the sounds of the door banging open and footsteps on the stairs. But they never came. She ran to the window to see what was happening – and froze. There was nothing there. The drive stood empty. When she turned back to the cradle, the baby had died.

Many years later, when the child's father was searching through some old deeds and papers, he found an old letter that said that if the heir were to die at Littlecote then the spirit of 'Wild Will' Darrell would come to take them away.

This story is one of the best known of all Wiltshire tales, and perhaps the nastiest. In addition to Mother Barnes's statement, a letter from Sir Henry Knyvett, husband of the slandered Lady Knyvett, written in 1578 and detailing Darrell's ill deeds, was unearthed at Longleat in the 1870s. The story left its fair share of ghosts behind. Darrell still haunts the stile where he died, fleeing the hounds of Hell that pursue him, he rides in a haunted coach, and he can also be seen in the bedchamber. The mother and the baby have been seen in the bedchamber as well, and Mother Barnes has been seen kneeling by the hearth.

12

JACK-O'-
THE-LANTERN

It was well known across the Downs that Old Jacob was the finest shepherd yet living, and his dog Tan was considered to be nearly as wise as his master. For fifty years Old Jacob had been frozen, baked and soaked with his sheep up on the Downs, and for a good twelve of those Tan had been at his side. But both Jacob and Tan were getting on in years, and Farmer Farley, who had inherited Jacob as an employee along with the farm twenty-five years ago, was getting worried about the future.

'You'll have to learn up a lad,' said Old Jacob when Farley broached the matter. 'I'll see him right, if you'll let me, and Tan'll see to the dog, right enough. And if they don't want to learn, then I'll still see 'em taught – for the sheep, y'understand – the hard way.'

So word was put out that Farmer Farley needed a shepherd and Old Jacob was going to train him. Applications came in thick and fast for the chance to work with the master, and Farmer Farley asked around the villages to see who looked promising. He decided on a young lad who'd won a few competitions down in the valleys with his young bitch.

Tom was as proud as a cow with two tails to be chosen. He and his bitch, Fan, strutted up to the farm on Monday morning as full of themselves as if they were going up to the podium to collect another rosette. Old Jacob gave them both a good long look and then, with Farmer Farley looking on, he asked young Tom to round up a flock of twenty sheep.

It was all over in five minutes, the sheep quivering in a huddle in the pen, and Fan yipping and dancing for the sheer joy of it. Tom looked prouder than ever as he strutted back to Old Jacob.

'That'll do, won't it?' he said. 'Fan's a fast 'un.'

But Old Jacob was shaking his head.

'All bark and bustle,' he said. 'Sheep don't like hustle – and they don't forget, so you're going to find 'em harder to herd now.'

Tom sneered and was about to reply when Farmer Farley asked Old Jacob to show them all how it was done. Jacob whistled to Tan, who stretched, then ambled over to sit at his master's feet. Softly, Jacob spoke to the dog and told him to go in the pen and fetch out the lame ewe from the middle of the flock.

The sheep were nervous, and jostling in all directions at once, but Tan just strolled in, as gentle as you like. The flock began to relax and nibble at the grass. For a moment Tan seemed to disappear amidst the white bodies, but then he was out again, a limping ewe hobbling along in front of him, and the other sheep didn't even lift their heads as they passed.

Old Jacob laid a gentle hand on Tan's head, then checked the ewe's foot and eased out the thorn that pained her. Only when that was done did he look up at the red-faced boy.

'Boys and puppies is all a'scramble, but sheep ain't – they like it slow and steady.'

It wasn't the best beginning. Tom and Fan were used to praise not criticism. Tom nursed his anger over a pint or two that evening in the pub and gritted his teeth when people congratulated him on his good fortune in winning the apprenticeship. It didn't get any better. Tom thought Old Jacob was slow and stupid. Fan didn't like Tan much either. The older dog was slow too and preferred to snooze in the autumn sunshine than race or tussle. He was dull, dull, dull.

Old Jacob didn't seem too worried that the training was slow, but Farmer Farley fretted that the winter looked to be a hard one

and that Jacob's chest wasn't as strong as it used to be, and that
Tom and Fan were still rushing the flock and unsettling them. The
flock were so keyed up that they jumped at anything, and only
Tan's calm presence would ease them.

'Will they shape well enough, Jacob?'

Old Jacob smiled. 'Don't you go worrying now. The winter'll
learn 'em if I can't teach 'em, just as it taught me, when I was a
young pup and cocksure myself.'

'I reckon they'll be learning the hard way,' said Farmer Farley.

Jacob nodded. 'And it'll not be long now, neither.'

With that Farmer Farley had to be content.

He was right, it was a hard winter. The snow fell and fell from
January on and didn't stop, save to freeze. Fan got more useful in
the cold weather as she was less inclined to race about in the chill,
and she even consented to huddle up by the fire with Tan, but Tom
still pushed her and got her excited. It was almost wilful, but Jacob
noted how kind the young man's hands were when he handled the
sheep when he thought the old man wasn't looking.

It was still snowing when the ewes came to lamb. It would
usually be Tan who went to round up the flock, but the dog's poor
old joints were stiff, and Jacob's chest didn't sound so good. Farmer
Farley sent the boy and Fan to bring them in, while Jacob and Tan
stayed in the sheep hut with the birthing ewes.

Tan was put to keeping two orphan lambs safe and warm with
his body heat, and Jacob felt old as he listened to the wuthering
of the wind outside. In all his sixty years as a shepherd he'd never
lost a healthy sheep, but these twins had cost their mother her life.
Still, there were things to be done. He eased himself up and took
a pannikin of warm milk outside to set down out of the wind for
Jack-o'-the-Lantern.

He was greatly relieved when he heard Tom and Fan coming in
with the flock and went outside to check on them. Tom looked as
pleased as punch.

'Fan and me we've brought in twenty-one.'

Old Jacob's heart sank. It was some minutes before he let himself
speak.

'Twenty-one? As you well know, there should be twenty-four.'
He checked the flock. 'What about those three ewes that're close
to their time?'

Tom blustered about snow and fog and cold. Old Jacob just
stared at him.

'A man could die out there!' cried Tom.

'Well then, you just get out there and die finding 'em. You're no
shepherd yet, so you'll learn the hard way. Tan'll go with you – he's
saved ewes in worse snows than this – and I'll follow along with a
lantern when this one's done her birthing. Now go.'

For a moment Tom just stood there, reeling from what Jacob
had said, and then the anger rose in him. He was frozen to the
bone, his feet were numb from tramping through the snow and he
was hungry and tired. But he took the two dogs and went back out
into the snow and fog.

When he thought he was out of view, he turned and gave Tan
a vicious kick. The dog yelped, and Fan whimpered in sympathy
and clung close to her master's leg. But Tan, as quick as you like,
he turned about and gave Tom's leg a good slash with his teeth and
then, without another sound, went ahead to find the ewes.

But Tom was wrong. Someone had seen them, and seen that
kick. Sitting on the roof of the sheep hut sat Jack-o'-the-Lantern,
waiting for the kerfuffle to die down so he could drink up his
pannikin of milk before it got cold. Now, Jack liked Old Jacob,
for he always made sure Jack had fresh milk. That boy was another
thing, and that Fan had got to the milk once. Jack grinned to
himself in anticipation, leapt from the roof and disappeared.

The way was hard, and it would have been hard enough with
just the snow, but the fog turned the familiar hills into unknown
mountains. Tom was in such a mood that he didn't care.
He stamped along seeing nothing but the black thoughts inside his
own head, and neither he nor Fan noticed that Tan was no longer
there.

After he'd blundered about in a rage for a while, Tom realised
he had to find the ewes before he dared go home, so he and Fan
searched until they were blue with cold. But they found nothing

in the darkness. When Tom at last saw Old Jacob's lantern winking ahead of them he didn't care that the old man would berate him or that he might lose his position. He was just glad to go after him to get home.

The old man was moving at a fair whack, though, and no matter how fast Tom went he couldn't catch up with him. He called out to him to stop, but he just kept going. Suddenly, Tom felt a creaking under his feet, then he crashed into icy water up to his knees and poor Fan was in up to her shoulders and howling.

The light winked out.

Tom and Fan stood alone in the icy water and the whirling snow and, to their surprise, they heard laughter echoing through the valley. Fan whimpered and crushed close to her master. Tom knew then that the laugh – and the light – came from no human thing.

They were both exhausted by the time they made it back to the sheep hut. But there was no welcome for them, only Farmer Farley in a fine fury. Tom tried to explain about the ewes and the lambs and how they hadn't found them, but Farmer Farley cut him short.

'Well, it's just as well that Tan found them right by the gate, isn't it? Though he found that hard enough with a sore muzzle, didn't he? My Lass had to help out and only just in time to save those lambs. You should know better than to hurt another man's dog, so I reckon you'd best get inside and learn your lesson the hard way.'

Tom listened with his head hung low. Then he squared his shoulders and was just about to go inside when he heard a laugh above him. He looked up and saw a light wink on just above the sheep hut. He shot inside. All he said to Old Jacob was a mumbled 'Sorry'. Jacob nodded, set a bowl of warm milk down for poor shivering Fan, and then gave Tom a good leathering with his belt. When that was done, he pressed a bowl of porridge into the boy's hands and said, 'You best eat that, unless you're warm enough already.'

And outside, on the roof, Jack-o'-the-Lantern laughed and laughed until Tom slipped out and set a brimming bowl of porridge down for him as well.

The Jack-o'-the-Lantern in this story is a spirit that lures foolish travellers – and shepherds – into boggy places to their doom. The phenomenon of ghostly lights in marshy areas might have a natural cause; it may be glowing decaying matter, or luminescent barn-owls, but none of the explanations sound that convincing to me! It has many names, including Will-o'-the-Wisp, Hinkypink, Friar's Lantern or Corpse Candle. The Jack-o'-the-Lantern is often thought to be an evil soul trapped on the earth after death, but the creature in this story seems more like a fairy taking revenge on an evil deed done to an innocent – the dog. The story was collected by Ruth Tongue.

13

THE MARE'S EGG

It was their first time to the country. The two young men had not even been to Hampstead Heath or Richmond Hill. The greenest place they'd seen in their lives was Hyde Park, and then only on high days and holidays. A weekend in the country seemed just the ticket. They'd stayed the night in an inn with a thatched roof, they'd drunk cider and they'd marvelled at the green everywhere. And they'd marvelled too at the locals with their slow and steady speech, their rough clothes and seamed faces, and thought themselves quite superior with their spivvy London suits and their horn-topped canes. Not that they'd ventured far. They were only staying in Hampshire. But the next day they decided to be adventurous, took the train to Grately, and walked out across the fields into Wiltshire.

They'd not gone very far when they spied an old man walking along the path towards them. They sniggered to each other as they took in his broad straw hat, his embroidered smock and his trousers tied with string below the knee. He carried a fat pumpkin under one arm – an object not in their repertoire of vegetables.

'Let's have some sport with this one, shall we?' whispered one to the other.

'Hey!' cried the other to the old man. 'What's that you're carrying, then?'

The old man looked at them long and slow. He took in the fancy suits, now liberally spattered with mud, the unsuitable shoes, the cocky hats and the horn-topped canes.

'This 'ere be a mare's egg,' he said.

The two young men looked at each other and frowned. But then, who were they to know whether a horse birthed babies – or hatched them? Best humour the man, they thought. So they praised the thing to the nines.

'Thank'ee, kind sirs,' said the old man. 'It's no common egg, y'see. There's plenty o' them about. No, this 'ere one's a thoroughbred.'

When the young men heard this, their eyes lit up. They imagined riches pouring in as their horse won victory after victory. They saw themselves surrounded by falling banknotes, riding in fine carriages with fancy girls and drinking champagne. They even imagined themselves as Prime Minister.

'How much do you want for it?'

Well, the old man hummed and hawed and sucked his remaining teeth and protested that he'd not like to lose the line, but after a while he came out with a sum that made the young men's eyes water.

'For a thoroughbred,' he said firmly.

So they set to bargaining, and eventually the young men beat him down to a price that satisfied everyone. Once the money was paid, the old man very gently laid the egg in one of the young men's arms.

'Take good care of she. She'll be hatching soon.' And then he was off at a surprisingly brisk pace.

'Must be the country air,' said one to the other. But then they realised how long they'd been haggling. It was nearly time for the last train home. So, with the egg cradled in one young man's jacket, they set off at a brisk trot across the fields towards the station. They heard the distant toot of the train's whistle and had to break into a run. Immediately, one of them tripped over a juniper bush, and – wouldn't you know it? – it was the one carrying the egg.

It shot out of his arms and rolled down the hill towards the railway line. They gave chase as fast as they could, but before they could reach it the egg thwacked hard into a hedge. They were horrified and saw their dreams of riches slipping away. But, as they stared, something shot out of the hedge and bolted across the next field. Something with four powerful legs, two long ears and a pale flash of tail.

'Our foal!' they cried, and gave chase. But the creature was far too fast. It quickly disappeared into the undergrowth and was gone.

Two very crestfallen young men got onto the train at Grately. The other passengers were puzzled to hear them say, over and other, 'If it was that fast as a little baby, how fast would it have been on the track?'

This story comes from John Egerton's Sussex Folk and Sussex Ways, *but describes a Wiltshire incident. It shows, once again, that the folk of Wiltshire are cannier than they are sometimes given credit for!*

14

SIR BEVIS
OF HAMPTON

There was once a fine manor house at Downton. The Earl of Southampton was its lord, and when he was in need of a wife he had the wealth to look among the highest maidens of the land. He chose the King of Scotland's daughter. They were married with great celebrations and he took her to live at his Wiltshire estate. But the King of Scotland's daughter was not content. She was a Princess, and could not bear to be married to a mere earl.

She did her wifely duty by her lord, but she gave him no love, and when a son was born to her she would not look at him. It was his father who named the boy Bevis, and as he grew Bevis was the apple of his father's eye. The King of Scotland's daughter hardly ever sent for him, and as a small child Bevis almost believed it was his nurse who was his mother.

When Bevis was seven years old, the King of Scotland's daughter took a lover: Sir Murdour, the brother of the Emperor of Germany. They schemed and plotted and planned, and when the time was right, they murdered the Earl. She set up her lover as the new Earl, then went to her Uncle Saber and demanded, 'Take the boy away and kill him. I can't bear to look at him.'

But when Bevis was delivered into Saber's hands, he found that he couldn't kill the boy. He dared not tell his niece. Instead he took

Bevis up on the Downs and, without saying who the boy was, gave
him into the care of a poor shepherd family. Saber bent down and
put his hands on Bevis's shoulders.

'You must abide,' he said, 'and grow up safe and strong, and then
we shall see what we shall see.'

Bevis understood. But as he grew he would go and sit out on the
Downs with his sheep where he could look down into the grounds of
Downton Manor. He would watch the lords and ladies walking there
and hear their laughter, until he burned with anger. And with his
shepherd's crook he practised the moves he remembered his father's
men-at-arms doing in the courtyard.

One day, when he was eleven years old, the rage built in him so
much that he snapped. He ran down the hill and was in the manor
before anyone could stop him. Sir Murdour sat at the high table,
and the rage burnt in Bevis so fiercely that he flew at the knight
with his shepherd's crook and struck him to the ground.

The King of Scotland's daughter screamed.

'Seize him!'

Men leapt from the shadows, grabbed him and pushed him to
the floor so hard that his head cracked against the ground.

When he awoke, it was dark and the ground moved beneath
him. He tried to jump up, but his feet and his hands were tied.
The place reeked of human filth – but under that was the tang of
salt. He was on a ship. As his eyes grew accustomed to the dark, he
made out other people slumped against the curved hull.

'What's happening?' he cried. 'Where are they taking us?'

But the people only wept and wailed.

They disembarked at a city where the sun shone so bright that it
blinded him. Tall domed palaces glittered with colour and strange
cries echoed through the streets. His captors shouted in a strange
tongue and cracked whips at them as they stumbled onto the quay.
He realised that he had been sold into slavery.

His captors dragged him to the marketplace and scrubbed him
so that his pale skin shone and his yellow hair gleamed. Then the
bidding began. Merchants and traders all clustered around this
exotic pearl. But it just so happened that the King of that land was

in the marketplace that day, and when he saw the boy with the yellow hair he knew he had to have him as a slave.

The King watched his new young slave over the next few months and was pleased with what he saw. The boy soon learned their language, he was quick to read and figure in this new tongue. The King made Bevis his page. Bevis had to follow the King everywhere, running errands and carrying things for him. So he was there when the King visited his only child, Josian.

Josian was fascinated by the pale slave. She begged her father, 'Please, let him stay and take his lessons with me.'

The King doted on his only child. He couldn't refuse her. From then on Bevis and Josian were inseparable. He poured out his story to her, and his longing to go home, and she confided her loneliness at being the King's daughter. You'd often see them squeezed into a nook together, one golden and one dark head bent over a book of poetry, or you'd see them playing catch in the gardens. No one thought anything of it, for children are children whether slaves or princesses.

But children don't remain children forever. As they grew up Bevis and Josian discovered that the poetry they read together began to make more sense, and they looked at each other with eyes of love.

The King remained oblivious. He cherished Bevis almost as if he were his son. When Bevis was old enough, he sent him to be trained as a knight, and gave him his arms himself. But the other knights hated him for his pale beauty and the Princess's favour. When they got him alone, they would mock him and knock him about.

'Slave-boy!' they called him.

'Ghost-boy! Pale and puny and sickly – just like a ghost!'

'Where's your father's land now?' they would cry, pushing him between them. 'With your mother and her lover?'

And just as he had when he was a boy, Bevis felt the rage in him build and build until he was ready to burst. But now he didn't have just a shepherd's crook. As the rage roared he drew his sword and he cut them down. He killed sixty knights that day in the heat of his fury. When he realised what he'd done, he fell to his knees and he wept. Then he went to the King and told him what had happened.

The King was furious, and a little frightened. Where had the boy got such strength, such skill? And how could the boy do this to him after all he'd given him?

'He must die!' he cried.

But Josian begged her father to let him live. If he had heard the endless taunting, she argued, he would have understood.

'Surely you have some task you can set him, Father, so he can atone for what he has done.'

The King thought about it, for he could still refuse her nothing, and remembered that far to the east lived a great boar that was the terror of the land. No knight he had sent to dispatch it had ever returned.

'If you kill the boar,' said the King to Bevis, 'then your killings will be forgotten – and there may be a reward for you.'

Bevis bowed his head. He'd heard of the boar, and the lost knights, and he understood that the King didn't want him to come back. But when he went to say a final farewell to Josian, she slipped her hand into his and said, 'Follow me.'

She led him down to the stables, and beckoned him towards a stall. Inside was a fine chestnut stallion with a silver mane and tail. Bevis ran his hand over the beast's smooth flank and was lost.

'He's yours,' whispered Josian.

'I shall name him Arundel,' said Bevis, 'after a fine castle in my father's land that I visited once as a boy.'

'I have another gift.' From beneath her skirts, Josian drew a long sword. 'This is Morglay. I had it made for you.'

Bevis took the sword, and it balanced in his hand as if it were an extension of his arm. He embraced and kissed Josian in thanks, then mounted Arundel and rode away to face the boar.

He found the great boar's den in the middle of a great forest. The floor of the den was scattered with the bones of men. The beast was enormous. Each of his tusks alone was the length of a man's leg. But Bevis was not afraid. All day he fought the beast, till at last he thrust Morglay up through its mouth and cut its heart in two. He cut off the boar's head and carried it home to present to the King.

The King was amazed at what Bevis had done. The sixty knights were forgotten. Instead, the King asked Bevis to name his reward.

He expected the young man to ask for his freedom and a passage home to his cold northern land, but Bevis had other plans.

'I would have as my reward your daughter's hand in marriage.'

The King could not believe his ears.

'What snake have I nurtured at my breast these long years? Marry my daughter, my Josian? No, that shall never be!'

But Josian spoke up. 'Father, I love him and would have him as my husband. He killed the great boar! Is he not worthy?'

The King looked at Bevis and remembered the love he had for him. But to let a slave marry his only child? Rule his kingdom once he was gone? He looked at Josian and saw her love for Bevis. How could he refuse her? But he had to be strong.

'Unless you consent to convert to our religion, you may never marry her.'

In his heart, Bevis still longed for England and the manor at Downton. He knew he would never see them again if he renounced his god.

'I cannot do that,' he said.

'Very well,' said the King. For a moment he was tempted to have the young man hauled away and killed to remove the problem, but then another solution came to him. 'I have recently heard that my great enemy, Bradmond, the King of Syria, has sailed his ships to our borders and threatens our lands. Take a body of men and see him off, and I might consider your request.'

So Bevis rode with the King's army to the coast, and met Bradmond's army on the plain. Despite having never commanded an army before, Bevis soon defeated Bradmond with his cunning and skill. Bradmond and his men fled back to their ships and sailed away. When Bevis got back to the palace his request was just the same.

'I would have as my reward your daughter's hand in marriage.'

The King tried another tack. 'You may marry my daughter, for all you are an unbeliever, if you promise never to try to go back to this England of yours. I must have a man I can rely on to rule well after me.'

Bevis longed to go home. He looked to his love but Josian, who had listened to him speak of his home so many times as they were growing up, shook her head. She would not make him give up his dream.

'I cannot do that,' he said and hung his head in despair.

That night Josian crept to his rooms and told him that she loved him and that they should run away together. She'd heard so much about Downton and Wiltshire that she longed to see them and could think of nothing better than to be his lady in his land.

But, like all rulers, the King had spies. One of Josian's young maids whispered in the King's ear that his daughter was planning to elope.

The King was furious. He sent for Bevis. He hid his fury with a smile and embraced him. 'I have been thinking', he said, 'that I should listen to my daughter. You are a fine knight and would make her a fine husband. But there is one last thing you must do for me. You must deliver a letter into the hands of my enemy Bradmond. You must go as a humble slave, to flatter him, so you must not take your horse or your sword.'

When Josian heard of this, she begged Bevis not to go. 'Can't you see it's a trick?'

But Bevis shook his head.

'I would rather that we were married with honour. Besides, all I have to do is deliver a letter. What harm can there be in that? Don't worry. I'll be home before you know it.'

So he sailed away to Damascus. When he arrived, he handed Bradmond the letter, and the King opened it and read what it said. There was just one line. When Bradmond read it he burst out laughing.

The letter said, 'Kill the bearer.'

'Clap him in irons and throw him in the pit!' cried Bradmond. Bevis had no sword. The guards wrestled him to the ground and dragged him away. They carried him beyond the walls of the castle, and there they opened a great door in the ground and flung Bevis in.

Bevis smacked his head as he landed on the hard ground and knew no more. When he awoke, he saw the walls of his prison stretch high and smooth above him. There were two recesses to either side, shading into darkness. As he peered into one, two lights winked on. He wheeled around to the other, and saw two more.

Eyes! There were eyes in the darkness. He staggered to his feet.
There were beasts on either side him, and he could see nothing but
their eyes. Then a coil of flame rolled across him.

Dragons! He had been thrown into a pit of dragons.

The creatures leapt, but Bevis was ready. He caught the beasts by
their necks, and for a long day and a long night they struggled. But
finally, with a great heave, he twisted them together, twisted them
around each other, till their necks snapped and the dragons fell
dead at his feet. But Bevis was still trapped.

As Josian waited for her lover to return, her fear grew with every
passing day.

At last, after a year had passed, her father came to her and said,
'My dear, he has left you. It was only to be expected, and that is
why I tested him. Give him freedom and a little gold in his pocket
and a slave will always run. He'll be back in his homeland by now,
and I wish him well, but be assured he thinks no more of you.
It's time that you were married.'

Josian swore she would never marry and that Bevis would
return, but her words counted for nothing. Before the month was
out, her father had wed her to King Inor of Morbraunt. This King
looked at his new bride and his lip curled. He saw her defiance.

'Bring out that horse, Arundel!' he cried.

Arundel was brought, dragging his hooves and squealing. He had not let anyone on his back since Bevis left. His eyes rolled in fury as the grooms dragged him near. Inor smiled at Josian.

'My dear,' he said, 'I will break you just as I break this horse.'

Inor leapt on Arundel's back, and Josian watched as the horse bucked and kicked and screamed. For a moment Arundel calmed, and her heart began to sink, but then the stallion bucked and Inor flew from his back. She waited till the doctors came to her and proclaimed him dead, and then she gently led the horse away.

Six more years passed, and still Bevis languished in the pit. But his guards had grown tired of the bother of feeding him, and tired of waiting for him to die. The first Bevis knew of it was that the great door creaked open and he saw a rope dangling above him. As he watched the men lowered themselves down, their swords at the ready.

He didn't stop to think. He leapt onto the rope and squirmed up it, seized their swords and cut them down. They fell into the pit, and Bevis climbed to top and ran.

He made his way back to take Josian for his own. Great was his despair when he heard she had got married. Great was his relief when he heard she was widowed and ruling her husband's land. He made his way to Morbraunt and, disguised as a Christian pilgrim, asked to be admitted to her palace.

To his surprise the guards took him there straight away. He stood in the hall with the other supplicants and waited. At last she came down the stairs and his heart leapt. She was just as beautiful as before, but he saw that her beauty had been tempered with new strength. She looked around the hall and when her eyes lit on the Christian she walked straight up to him and folded a small package into his hands.

'Go well, pilgrim. I give you these alms in memory of a Christian knight I once loved.'

When he heard this, Bevis threw back the hood of his robe. Josian let out a small cry and flung herself into his arms. Before anyone could say a word they fled from the hall and ran down to the stables where Arundel was waiting.

They had many adventures on their journey: giants, dragons, betrayal, separation and reunion. But at last Bevis set foot again in his father's land, and marvelled at its fertile greenness. They went straight to his mother's Uncle Saber, where the old man welcomed him with tears and thanks to the Lord.

'Your mother still rules at Downton,' he said, 'with Sir Murdour at her side. Take my men and do what you will with my blessing.'

So Bevis took his uncle's men and rode to the manor at Downton. When he reached his childhood home, the tears fell freely as he remembered all that had been done to him. Then he called out to Sir Murdour to show his face and fight.

Murdour brought out his knights and there was a great battle. Bevis fought with a strength and power that no man could withstand. He cut his way through to the centre, where Murdour was protected by his knights, and challenged him. Murdour was white with fear, but he had no choice but to agree, and they fought until Murdour lay dead on the field. When word was carried to the King of Scotland's daughter, she screamed and ran to the top of the highest tower and cast herself off it to her death.

At last, Bevis entered his own hall and the men bowed down to the true Earl of Southampton. There at Downton he and Josian were wed, and there they spent the rest of their days. After her own desert land, Josian thought that green Wiltshire was very exotic indeed.

Bevis of Hampton is one of England's most famous medieval romances. There are many different versions. The story seems to have first been written in medieval French around 1200, but translated into Middle English in the late thirteenth century. The poem is 4,620 lines long and ranges from England to Albania, Syria and Germany. The village of Downton, right on the Wiltshire border with Hampshire, was the site of the Earl of Southampton's residence in the story. Downton is less than twenty miles from Southampton.

15

THE GHOST OF MANTON BARROW

By the beginning of the twentieth century the round barrow at Manton was a mess. The plough had been over it so many times that you could hardly see it was round. It was a wreck even before the plough got to it because, despite the tales that warned of dire punishments awaiting hill-diggers, there were many who were happy to try their luck searching for gold. But they never found any at Manton.

They say that the dead were put in barrows to guard the boundaries, to watch the land and to protect the living. This barrow was carefully placed halfway up the hill overlooking the River Kennet, to watch the trade and folk coming up and down the river.

In 1906 the barrow was disturbed once more when an archaeologist arrived. Maud Cunnington had been excavating in the area for about ten years. Her major discoveries at Woodhenge, Stonehenge and Avebury were yet to come. In those days, it was so unusual to see a female archaeologist that Maud had to work under her husband's name; the finds from the dig are duly recorded as found by Howard B. Cunnington. Often they worked together, but at Manton Maud did the work.

The excavation was carefully planned. First, they mapped out the barrow and the ditches that had once ringed it. The centre was identified. A trench was laid from the south-west and digging began. Many of the older villagers shook their heads and muttered to each other, but there were enough locals happy to risk the ghosts for money in their pockets. Maud and these local helpers sifted the earth as the trench neared the centre, but there was nothing in the finds around the edge to suggest what they would find in centre.

Exactly in the middle they found a grave. In it lay a crumbling skeleton, and scattered around the bones lay what all those barrow thieves hoped for – treasure. The burial turned out to be the richest prehistoric grave to have been found in Wessex. Investigation showed the corpse was a woman, but no young maid. She was a mature woman, her limbs aching with arthritis, but rich and powerful. She was buried with evidence of her status all around her: rare gold from Ireland, hammered thin over beads, shaped into a tiny halberd pendant, and a disc like the shining sun; there was jet from Yorkshire, a whole finely polished necklace of it; and a large chunk of amber from the Baltic, traded across the rivers and seas of Europe and set into the pommel of a bronze dagger.

When she died they laid her on a finely woven woollen cloth and draped another over her. They burnt incense to mask the smell of death. They piled earth over her to raise a barrow twelve feet high and more than sixty feet across. She was a powerful woman indeed.

The wonderful finds were packed up and sent to Maud's husband, who was the honorary curator at Devizes Museum, but the skeleton wasn't needed. It was left behind in the care of Mr Bucknell, the owner of Barrow Cottage nearby. Who knows what Maud told him? 'Keep it safe while we decide what to do about it'? 'Don't show it to anyone'? Whatever she said, Mr Bucknell ignored it. He showed the skeleton to anyone who paid him a penny, and for a little bit extra...

A journalist all the way from London came seeking a story, and after slipping an extra bob or two to Mr Bucknell, he went back to London with his prize. He took the bone he had borrowed to a well-known medium, and a séance was organised. The room was

gloomy in the flickering candlelight. The medium sat at the head
of the table. All around her, hand clutched sweaty hand as the
journalist and his friends avidly waited for the spirit to appear.

The medium began to moan and sway from side to side, and
one by one the candles flickered and died until just three were
alight, illuminating the medium's rolling eyes and heaving bosom.

'She's coming,' she groaned, and then sat up straight. Her eyes
flicked open, then rolled up so that only the whites showed, and a
slow smile spread across her face.

'I am Elfrida, and I was just a girl when they took me – my own
uncle's men! We were new in this land, and things were not good.
Those Welsh attacked our little farms and killed my family and
friends. It seemed our gods had deserted us in this new land, so my
uncle, the chief, and his men knew there had to be a sacrifice, and
there I was, fatherless, alone and young, just seventeen. They took
me to the hill and they cut my throat for Woden. I would have my –'

The medium suddenly slumped forward and lay on the table like
one dead. The journalist broke free and ran to get a glass of water,
which he pressed to her lips. Soon she was blinking and smiling
nervously at the young man. No, she didn't remember what she'd
said. It was always like that when the spirits came...

A Saxon Princess sacrificed to Woden! It was a cracking story
and the press loved it, but back in Wiltshire no one paid much
attention. The Cunningtons were too busy researching the Bronze
Age barrow finds to be bothered by such tosh, and Mr Bucknell
was just glad to get his bit of bone back.

He had troubles of his own. They started when a friend came
over from America, and Bucknell couldn't resist giving him a little
something.

'A little souvenir of home,' he said as he pressed the little finger
bone into his friend's hand and closed his fingers over it with a
smile and a wink.

The friend pocketed the bone, thanked Bucknell and went off
back to America. Bucknell thought no more about it. But not long
afterwards, as winter came in, he found one of his hands starting
to ache. The tips of his fingers were always cold and nothing

would keep them warm, but even worse was when feeling in them disappeared altogether and the tips started to go black. He tried to ignore it, but when the little finger was black right down to the first joint, he crept off to the doctor's in Marlborough. The doctor packed him straight off to hospital and the whole offending finger was quickly removed.

The doctors said that they were going to throw the finger away, but Bucknell had other ideas. When he saw the finger, so like the one he had given away, he knew what he had to do. So he shook his head.

'I'll keep it,' he said, 'as a souvenir.'

When he got home, he found instructions had come from the Cunningtons in Devizes to rebury the body. Bucknell took the bones to the barrow and carefully laid them out just as they had been discovered, and then, with great solemnity, placed his own finger bone in place of the one that was missing. Then he shovelled the earth back in till she was good and gone, and walked away as fast as he could.

But that wasn't the end of it. A while later, another Marlborough doctor, Dr J.B. Maurice, was called to see an old woman who lived not far from the barrow. When he got there, she was standing in her doorway, wringing her hands.

'Every night,' she said, 'since that woman from Devizes came and disturbed the old creature she's come out of the mound and squinny in the window. I do hear her most nights and want you to give me summat to keep her away.'

The doctor was a modern man of the world, but he knew his charges well. He hid a smile and rooted around in his bag, clicking the glass bottles one by one until he found the one he was looking for. Once unstoppered it gave off a heady scent.

'Take a wine glass of this – full up to the brim, mind – before you go to bed tonight, and then turn out all the lights and go to sleep in the dark. She'll think you're not there and she'll not trouble you anymore, mark my words.'

The old woman thanked him, and after a full glass of that heady stuff she felt much mellower – and calm enough to put out all the lights. She felt her way up to her bedroom in the darkness and

got under the covers, drew them up to her chin, and waited. Sure enough, she heard the scratching at the window, but in the darkness she couldn't see the old face peering through. She soon drifted into a deep and happy sleep. The 'old creature' didn't come back.

But what was the old creature after? Was she searching for her lost treasure? Her lost finger? Or had she awoken to find her land utterly changed, her precious grave goods stolen and everything different? Was she simply seeking companionship in an old woman not so unlike herself?

The excavation of Manton Barrow was one of the most important Bronze Age discoveries in Wessex in the early twentieth century. The folklore that has grown up around the barrow must have happened quite quickly, suggesting that people were a little unnerved by the finds. The 'old creature' is still buried in the barrow, but seems to be sleeping quietly now as no further sightings are known. The séance and the 'old creature' squinnying at the window come from Ben Cunnington, the archaeologist's husband, and Mr Bucknell's tale from L. V. Grinsell.

16

THE DEATH OF GUINEVERE

It was a dark night, lit only by the orange glow of a couple of pipes. There were three shepherds up on the Wansdyke that night: Tod Beake, an old hand; George Tasker, who was learning the trade well; and the lad. They huddled together for warmth and to keep out the blackness of the night. The only thing they could make out was the hulk of Tan Hill dark against the sky. Nearby, they could hear the crop, crop, cropping of grass by the sheep in the great ditch below them. Further off, a plaintive bleat was answered in kind. They had 300 sheep scattered on the Downs that night.

The men sat in companionable silence. Any efforts the lad had made at conversation had been answered with a brisk 'yes' or 'no' by the older men, and now even he had settled into a sleepy watchfulness.

'What's that?'

Tod's voice cut through the darkness. George and the lad started fully awake. The lad opened his mouth to say something, then shut it again as he heard it too. Men's voices, low and mournful, singing in some foreign lingo. Then came the snort of a horse, the chink of a bridle-bit, and the squeak of a wheel.

The shepherds looked at each other and, without a word, scrambled to their feet. Above, the clouds were thinning and the moon glowed through them.

'Many people come along here at night?' mumbled the lad.

Tod shook his head and whispered, 'Not often, lad. Not often.'

The moon came out and there, coming along the Wansdyke, was a party of men. At the front a man led two horses and a wagon, and around the wagon were ranged another six men. These six were the singers; they were dressed in long gowns and their bald crowns gleamed in the moonlight. They looked like monks.

'Bloody Catholics!' whispered George, nudging the lad.

But as the procession approached they took in other details. The man at the front was wore a strange long tunic to his knees and a thick cloak to his ankles, and his unfashionably long, grey hair fell over his shoulders. George glanced down at his own knee-breeches and coat and frowned. The horse's tack looked odd, too, and as the wagon drew closer they saw it carried a coffin, and on the coffin glinted a circle of gold.

Suddenly George caught his breath. For he'd seen that neither the men's feet nor the horses' hooves touched the ground. Instead they drifted an inch or two above it. He glanced at his friends and saw that they too had realised what he now knew. These were no mortal men. This was a party of ghosts.

The lad gave a cry, and fled, and he never stopped running till he'd run all the way down to Bishop's Cannings. But George and Tod stayed beside the Wansdyke and watched the procession draw near.

When Arthur fell at the Battle of Camlann, it pitched the land into chaos. All the King had worked for, those long years of holding the petty chiefs of Britain together, fell apart in an instant. There was a scramble for the High Kingship and wars broke out across the land. The Saxons that Arthur had held off throughout his reign now surged forward again, and chiefdom after chiefdom fell to the invaders. On top of that, the land mourned the King and the rain didn't stop falling all summer, leaving the crops in ruins and the people starving. Guinevere, Arthur's Queen, looked at all that had happened and blamed herself. If it had not been for her adultery her husband would still rule, and if it had not been for her barrenness, he would have had an heir.

She went to the nunnery at Amesbury, which had been founded by Arthur's uncle Ambrosius Aurelianus all those years ago, after the Night of the Long Knives. But she soon found that you can't run and you can't hide, either from those who love you or from yourself. When Lancelot found out where she had gone, he went immediately to Amesbury. He didn't know exactly what he was going to say, but he knew that when he left it would be with Guinevere at his side.

When he entered the courtyard where she and her maidens sat, she fainted dead away. When she came round and saw him bending over her, she held out her hand to stop him speaking.

'I know why you have come,' she said, 'but I cannot go with you. Not now and not ever. I will stay here and keep his memory alive. It is my dearest wish that I never see your face again in this life. This is my oath. Please, go and leave me be.'

When Lancelot tried to speak, she held up her hand again, and when she spoke again her voice was full of sorrow.

'It is my hope for you that you will go and live the life of an ordinary lord; the life you have denied yourself all these years. Take a wife. Have children. Rule your land. Please, go and do all these things. Go now, and think no longer of me.'

Lancelot bowed his head. He knew he had no choice but to accept her words, but he couldn't leave without one final kiss. He lowered his face to hers, but she turned her face away.

Although he left her then, he couldn't do what she'd asked. He had loved her too well and too long to ever love another. He was an old man now; best to leave loving to the young. He would take a different path. He couldn't be with her in the flesh, but he could be with her in spirit, so he went to Glastonbury and begged the Abbot to let him be a hermit in the abbey grounds.

When they found out, his friends went and begged him to return to the world. His fighting skill was needed. The chiefs respected him. But Lancelot would not listen. When they saw how he was living, they pleaded with him to stop punishing himself, to stop wearing a hair shirt, not to beat himself with the scourge, and to eat something other than bread and water, but to no avail.

For a year, Lancelot prayed for forgiveness. Then, one night, he had a dream. An angel came to him with wings outstretched in glory and said, 'Lancelot, we have one last task for you in this world. The Queen is dying. Go now to Amesbury and her bring here. Bury her here at Glastonbury.'

Lancelot awoke knowing that Guinevere was dying. He leapt up and, instead of dressing in his monk's habit, he put on his fine embroidered tunic, his long blue cloak and his tooled leather boots. He shook his long grey hair free of its binding, went to the Abbot and begged leave to go.

The Abbot saw the truth in his face and let him go. He told him to take six of the monks and bring the Queen back for burial. Lancelot wasted no time. The seven men rode furiously all day across Somerset and over the Downs to Salisbury Plain.

It was dusk when he hammered at the gates of the nunnery. He was swiftly let inside. But no sooner had he got inside than he heard wailing, and he knew he was too late. Two of the Queen's maidens came down the steps to greet him, their faces full of wonder.

'It is a miracle,' they said. 'For three nights she dreamt that you were coming, and for three days she has prayed that she might die

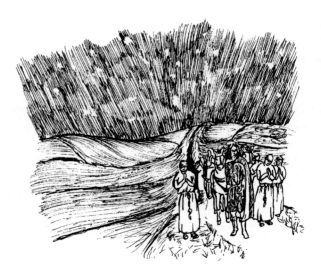

before you came, so that she would not break her oath. It is not an hour since she died.'

At that, Lancelot bowed his head and stood a little while, alone with his thoughts. Then he asked the maidens to take him to her. Her beauty was restored in death, all the care and lines smoothed away. He looked at her a long time, but could not weep. All his tears were long spent. Instead, he bent down and kissed her cold lips, then looked up at her maidens and told them he would lead the mass for her soul.

When this was done, and the Queen lowered safe into her coffin, Lancelot and his companions loaded her onto a wagon. So that the people would know who passed they placed her crown on the coffin. With Lancelot leading the way, they set out across the Downs to the Wansdyke, the monks singing for her soul as they carried her on to her final resting place.

As the cortège drew near, George saw there was so much grief in the man's face that even had he been a living man he would never have seen the two shepherds standing by the edge of the dyke. Tod gave George a sharp nudge and George saw him whip off his cap. George pulled off his own cap and bowed his head.

They stayed that way for a while, hearing the whickering of the horses and the low singing of the men. At last, as the music died away, George dared to look up. He was alone with Tod on the Wansdyke. The moon still shone and the Wansdyke stretched before them in both directions, but there was no sign of the procession and no sound except the sheep cropping the grass, the wind rustling the hedgerow in the field below and, far off, the low hooting of an owl.

The story was collected by Kathleen Wiltshire from Mrs Alice Maslen, whose grandfather was George Tasker. It is Wiltshire who suggests that the ghostly party might have been Sir Thomas Malory's story of Lancelot fetching back his beloved Guinevere from Amesbury.

17

THE ALDBOURNE
DABCHICK

It was a tranquil day in early spring. The waters of the village pond were smooth and the sky above shone fresh and blue. Only the church clock sounding the quarter-hour from the hill broke the silence. Farmers were long gone to the fields, and shepherds to tend the young lambs. Shopkeepers were sleepily setting out their wares on the street to the far side of the square. The hat-makers and the chair-bodgers were already at work, enjoying the sun which filtered through their windows.

Mrs Cor and her young son Michael were walking to the butcher's to get a pound of sausages. Michael dragged his mother to the pond's edge to see if the frogs had returned for the year. So he was the first to see it.

'Mum!' he cried. 'What's that?'

Mrs Cor turned to her son and studied the water. There was nothing to be seen but a few circular ripples.

'What's what, dear?'

'There was a bird there! Right there! It was just sitting there!'

As if in response, something popped up on the other side of the pond. A little brown bird with a fluffy rear bobbed calmly on the water. They could just see a glint of ruddiness about its throat.

'Where'd that come from?' Mrs Cor quickly made the sign against the Devil behind her back.

'That's it, Mum! But it was on this side before ... How'd it get over there?'

'What's all this then?' said Mr Fairchild, who kept a farm on the outskirts of the village.

'There's a strange bird in the pond,' began Michael.

'I don't see any bird,' said the farmer.

Michael turned round again. The bird had gone!

'It's a devil bird!' cried Mrs Cor.

Hearing her cry, other people began to come over to the pond. Soon there was a large circle of people watching the empty water.

'A bird, you say?' they shook their heads. 'There's no bird there.'

'There!' cried Michael. And there was the bird, right in the middle of the pond – small, innocent and brown. It opened its beak, and everyone held their breaths, and then –

'It's a horse!' cried someone. 'It's a horse in disguise!'

'A devil bird!' cried Mrs Cor again. 'I told you so!'

One of the village elders squinted closer. 'It's a bird alright,' he opined. 'The like of which I've never seen before.'

The hubbub grew. The bird looked at all the people and bobbed under again.

Everyone gasped and held their breaths. And kept on holding them. And kept on ... and on until they were fit to burst.

'It's killed itself!' cried Polly Wells, and burst into tears. The old ones shook their heads and started to turn away.

'Look!' cried Michael.

There was the strange little bird, looking none the worse for its adventure. Though half the village had turned out, nobody knew what it was.

'We should fetch old Will,' said someone from the back of the crowd.

'Yes! Old Will will know.'

Michael was sent to Old Will's house. His young daughter, Margaret, only eighty-two, answered the knock and listened to Michael's breathless request.

'But 'e's not left the house in years,' she quavered.

Michael ran around the back of the house and raced back with a wheelbarrow. Soon, Old Will was being pushed along faster than he'd moved for twenty years. When they reached the pond the crowds parted, and the bent old figure was wheeled to the water's edge. The bird, nibbling at something on the pond, seemed oblivious.

'It dived, you say?' asked Will. The crowd nodded.

'An' it come back?' asked Will. The crowd nodded again. Will ummed and ahhed and sucked his gums.

'You'd best wheel I around, and then I'll say.' So they wheeled him clockwise around the pond. All the while the bird sat tight. When they got back to where they'd started, Old Will sucked his gums again and said, 'Wheel I round again.' So they wheeled him widdershins.

'And again.'

So they wheeled him back clockwise. By the end of the third circuit, the villagers were all leaning in and Old Will seemed to realise he had to say something.

'I reckon,' he said, 'that it be nothing but a dabchick.'

Those fluffy-bottomed little diving birds have been known as 'dabchicks' in Aldbourne ever since. But when the folks of Ramsbury just down the road heard the tale, they laughed and laughed. They knew the bird well, for birds of that kind were common on the River Kennet that flowed nearby. The story confirmed what they had always suspected: Aldbourne folk were

fools. Every year after that at the annual Aldbourne feast, folks from Ramsbury would sneak in and tie a couple of the little birds, sadly dead, to the villagers' carts to surprise them on the way home.

But the people of Aldbourne didn't care. Much better to be an Aldbourne dabchick, they said, than to be a Ramsbury bulldog with black dogs on their roads, headless men bearing coffins near their pub, and the ghost of Wild Will Darrell in the church!

*A dabchick is a little grebe (*Tacybaptus rufucollis*). These small water birds are common on the Kennet but would have been an unusual visitor to Aldbourne's village pond. The derivation of the word 'dabchick' indicates that what Old Will was saying made a lot of sense. Not knowing what the bird was, he named it after a 'dab' or 'doppe' – Middle English for 'diving bird', and a 'chick' – a 'little bird'. So little grebes are indeed dabchicks. And they do make a noise rather like a horse's whinny.*

18

THE BATTLE OF EDINGTON

For three generations the Vikings had menaced the English. They came for treasure at first, raping and pillaging their way down the coastlines, forcing villages and monasteries alike to move inland. But by the ninth century, the Vikings had seen enough to know they wanted more. Not just England's gold, but its land. And more than that, they wanted power. They wanted to rule.

So they brought their armies and they attacked the kingdoms of England. Northumbria, already at war with itself, stood no chance against the invaders. By AD 866 Ivar the Boneless was ensconced in York, and the citizens of Northumbria paid their taxes to the Vikings.

East Anglia fell next. Its king, Edmund, was brutally murdered in AD 869.

In AD 874 it was Mercia's turn. King Burgred was routed in battle and went on the run. He fled across the Channel to the Continent to beg forgiveness of the Pope for deserting his people and abandoning them to Viking rule.

Only Wessex was left. The Vikings' eyes soon turned to the fairest land of all. Wessex, though, was a harder nut to crack. It had long had strong kings, who had fought and won against the

Vikings. When the Vikings first landed in Wessex, years before, old King Aethelwulf had held them off.

Aethelwulf was blessed with five sons, and one by one those sons became kings. But no one expected that the fifth son, Alfred, would ever be king. He was promised to the Church, and when he was only five years old was taken to Rome by his father and blessed by the Pope as his servant. While his brothers fought the Vikings, Alfred could be found poring over books or praying in the church. But one by one his brothers died, worn out by the constant fighting.

By the time Alfred was fifteen he only had one brother left: Aethelred. Alfred was named 'secundarius', the heir. He had to put aside his books and become a warrior.

He threw himself into this new role. Once, when he and his brother and the other nobles were celebrating mass before a battle, Alfred heard that fighting had begun outside the tent.

'Come, brother,' he whispered. 'Let us get to fighting!'

Aethelred stared at him. 'We can't interrupt the holy mass.'

Alfred rolled his eyes and leapt up. He pushed to the front of the sacrament queue, took the bread, and went out to gather his war band and enter the fray. His brother still sat inside the tent, waiting for the mass to finish. Alfred fought like a wild boar that day. When his brother emerged, the fight was nearly done.

By AD 870 Alfred was twenty-one and a seasoned warrior with a year of battles behind him. Some were defeats, but one was a great victory. At Ashdown, on the Berkshire Downs, he defeated the Viking host, and the Danish King Bagsecg and five Danish earls were killed. It seemed that Alfred would be a great commander. But in AD 871 Aethelred died and at only twenty-two, Alfred found himself king.

A young and untried king, a land in disarray; the Vikings saw their chance. While Alfred was still planning his brother's funeral, they surged into Wiltshire and defeated him. Days later they attacked again at Wilton, and again Alfred was defeated. He had no choice but to make peace. With the Vikings this did not mean sitting down and writing a treaty. Making peace with the Vikings meant you paid them money to go away.

For five years they left Alfred alone, but in AD 876 the Vikings got a new leader, Guthram the Dane. Guthram was not interested in honouring the agreements of his predecessors. He led a lightning attack into the heart of Wessex in late AD 877 and took the town of Wareham in Dorset. Alfred and his army tried to defeat them but could not, though they stopped the Vikings' advance.

Guthram backed down, and he and Alfred brought forward hostages, nobles from their own families, as assurance that their new treaty would hold. Guthram went on his knees in front of Alfred and swore on a ring dedicated to the god Thor, all the while staring up at Alfred with mocking eyes.

As soon as the ceremony was over and the King of Wessex gone, Guthram ordered the English hostages to be slain. The Vikings set off across the sea to Exeter. When Alfred heard of the killings he was furious. But he was no fool. He got to Exeter before the Vikings arrived and blockaded the port against them. Fate was on his side. A storm whipped up in the night and scattered the Viking ships. Again, Guthram had to surrender. Alfred didn't trust Guthram's word for a moment, but he wasn't in a strong enough position to continue the fight. He had no choice but to make peace again.

By now it was Christmas. Alfred went to his palace at Chippenham to celebrate the holy festival, secure in the knowledge that the fighting season was over for the year.

But he was wrong to feel secure. On Twelfth Night Guthram attacked the palace. Alfred was lucky to escape with his life. Guthram and his men settled down to attack the remains of the Christmas feast amid the devastation of the battle.

Alfred fled into the wilds of the Somerset Levels. That night, he took shelter in a peasant's hut and offended the wife by burning some cakes he'd been left to watch. Alfred apologised, but this failure seemed only to sum up all the others. But it made him see what he was fighting for: that people like this should always have enough – and feel confident enough to shout at strangers who did them wrong.

He sent word to his lords in Somerset, Wiltshire and Hampshire. He roved the land, whispering in people's ears, raising support.

Once he donned a singer's cloak and, in disguise, took a harp into Guthram's fortifications on the hill at Chippenham to sing for Guthram and to hear what plans the Vikings were making.

'You sing well,' said Guthram when the singer was done. 'Perhaps there is some merit in you English after all.'

Alfred smiled in thanks but said no more, and slipped away into the night with a map of Guthram's defences in his mind.

By Easter he had built a fortress at Athelney in Somerset, and by Whitsun he dared to step openly back into Wiltshire again as king. He chose as his rallying point Egbert's Stone on Kingsettle Hill, which looks out over the three counties of Somerset, Wiltshire and Dorset. From all directions men came. There was a great feeling of joy in the camp. It was almost as if their King had risen from the dead.

'Let us fight and take back what was lost!' cried Alfred. Some 4,000 men marched north. They camped the next night at Iley Oak and Alfred told them they would fight the next day. The two armies met on one of Alfred's estates, Edington. Alfred knew the land. He knew his men, too. They formed a great shield wall that the Vikings could not break, and over the long day pushed the invaders back. Guthram's army fell and the English chased him from the field, destroying the Vikings' cattle and capturing their horses. They chased them up to Chippenham, where Guthram and his men barricaded themselves into their fortifications. Alfred smiled grimly as he laid siege to his own land.

Within a fortnight the Vikings' food was gone and Guthram surrendered. He knew that this was the final defeat. Alfred knew this too, but he had learnt much since his early years as king. There were hostages and there were oaths, of course, but Alfred knew only too well about Guthram's oaths. He had another plan in mind.

'You will become a Christian,' he said. 'And I will be your godfather.'

So Guthram was brought into Alfred's family. Alfred understood that Guthram's honour would never allow him to double-cross his own kin. At the baptismal feast, Alfred called for music, and when none was forthcoming he took a harp himself and played. Guthram sat open-mouthed.

'You!' he cried when Alfred was done. 'You were the singer in our camp!'

Alfred bowed and smiled. Guthram knew he had truly met his match and he laughed and laughed and laughed.

It was a great victory, and Alfred wanted to commemorate it. Many times he had travelled through the Vale of the White Horse to the north and had seen the enigmatic beast that his ancestor Hengist had re-cut. What more fitting sign to show that the land was English through and through? Alfred took his men back to the site of the battle and there they carved a new horse, as white and crisp in the chalk as Hengist's.

When he stood at the base of Bratton Down and looked up at the gleaming white figure, Alfred laughed with joy. But he knew in his heart of hearts that although the Vikings were his friends now, there would always be more who would not honour his treaties. The Viking threat would be back.

So he prepared and prepared – and when the new threat came he was ready. But that's another story.

The existing Westbury White Horse was cut in 1778 by a Mr George Gee, but there are records from a few years before of a quite different horse, facing in the opposite direction, clearly male and with a crescent moon on the end of its tail. Was this Alfred's horse? The earliest mention of a horse, in 1742, dates its creation to within living memory. Given that debate rages between the Wiltshire and Somerset Edingtons over where the battle was fought, perhaps it was cut by some locals who wanted to demonstrate once and for all that Alfred's great victory was in Wiltshire. The Battle of Edington changed the course of England's history. Alfred and Guthram divided England up between themselves, creating the Danelaw. Critically, Alfred gained London. It is said that all the English outside the Danelaw now submitted to Alfred. It was the beginning of England as we know it today.

19

THE DEVIZES WIZARD

The Vicar of Wilcot was going mad. Night after night the church bells rang out and he could not get any rest. Night after night, they pealed as if a thousand couples were getting married, as if a thousand men had died, as if a thousand babies were being christened, as if it were Sunday morning and not the dead of night. The bells should have been a joyful sound, but not night after night, day after day, and not when no one believed you. Revd Palmer had taken to sleeping at the inn just to get the noise out of his head, because, you see, you could only hear the bells inside the rectory.

It all began a few years before, late one night in 1624. William Palmer, the Vicar of Holy Cross in Wilcot, was long abed. It was late enough that any civilised man or woman should have been fast asleep. But something made Palmer start awake. He sat up in bed, afraid, but then he heard words drifting up from outside:

'Holler the fox above them all, and cry as loud as you can call, whoop, whoop, whoop, whoop, whoop...'

He smiled grimly to himself and lay down again. Just another foolish drunk. Harmless enough. As the loud singing went on, an idea for Sunday's sermon formed in his mind. A little something on the evils of drink, perhaps?

Abruptly, the singing stopped and Palmer began to drift back to sleep. But it was only a brief respite, for he was jolted awake again almost immediately by a hammering at the front door. He wanted to assume it was the drunk and snuggle down under the sheets again, but what if it was something urgent? He couldn't take that risk.

He lit his candle and shuffled downstairs. The pounding didn't stop until he wrenched the door open and surprised the knocker with his fist held ready to beat it again. His heart sank as a gust of stale beer wafted towards him. It was the drunk, and no other. Indeed, it was a man he'd seen drunk many, many times. John Carter.

'What do you want?' Palmer strove to keep his voice civil.

'I wan' the keysh!' cried Carter. 'Wan' ring the bellsh! Cling clang!'

Palmer couldn't believe his ears.

'You want to ring the church bells? Now? It's the middle of the night, man!'

But Carter was shaking his head.

'Gotta ring the bellsh. Gimme the keysh to the church!'

Palmer pursed his lips.

'Pull yourself together, man,' he said. 'The ringing of the bells is a sacred and holy act to show our joy in God's work. I wouldn't give you the keys to the church even if it was bright daylight and you were stone-cold sober. Can you not see that it's late? Why, if I gave you the keys to the church and you rang the bells now, you'd awaken half the parish – not to mention Sir George himself, fast asleep in the house next door! Now get away with you!'

Carter wouldn't go. He started to get angry, shouting threats and demanding the keys over and over again. Palmer refused to listen any longer and slammed the door in the man's face. He locked it up tight and stamped back upstairs. For a few long minutes he listened to Carter promising revenge, but soon enough, deprived of his audience, the man went away.

The next day Palmer reported the incident to his patron, Sir George Wroughton, and the two men laughed over a glass of brandy. And that Sunday, the parishioners were treated to a sermon that dwelt heavily on the evils of drink. Palmer then dismissed the incident from his mind.

Carter, though, he thought on it. The tale, once told to Sir George, had filtered to his servants and was around the village in no time. Carter's friends continually came up to him and asked him if he'd ring the bells. The blacksmith actually got hold of a bell and followed him down the street with it. Even at church the Sunday after it happened, he'd heard the snickers as dreary Palmer droned on about the evils of liquor, and when the bells rang to mark the end of the service, well, it was all he could do to stop himself lashing out at his fellow villagers as they laughed. Palmer owed him, and owed him good, and Carter vowed he'd not rest until he'd had his revenge.

One day, a few weeks later, Carter was at the market in Devizes moaning about Palmer to anyone who'd listen over a pint or two. While he was paying the innkeeper, one of his friends sidled up to him and told him there might be someone who could help with his problem. Carter thanked his friend, and with ale-induced courage, he made his way down the back streets until he came to the address he'd been given. He knocked on the door, feeling the sweat trickle down his back, and looked around to see if anyone was watching. What he was doing was strictly illegal. His friend had given him the address of a wizard.

William Cantelow looked no different from any other man. His white collar was crisply starched and his black jacket freshly pressed. His long pale hair fell thin and wispy over his shoulders. But his eyes were different.

'Cold eyes, they were, that seemed to see right through you,' said Carter when he was safe back in the inn at Wilcot. 'It fair made me shiver, it did, and if I could have turned around and run, I reckons I would have done. But he invites me in, civil as you like, and he asks me what the trouble is. So I told him about that stiff-necked Vicar of ours, and he names a price. So I hands some money over, and he smiles and says, "Palmer of Wilcot is said to like bell ringing. Well, he shall have enough of that, I promise."'

From that day on Carter's revenge was sweet. The bells sounded in Palmer's house day-in, day-out till it came to the point the Vicar felt he was going mad. But you couldn't hear them outside, not even in Palmer's garden.

But it wasn't too long before Cantelow himself got his comeuppance. He'd got too bold, said one spell too many. He was slapped in Fisherton Gaol in Sarum, and there they forced a confession out of him.

'Yes, I caused the bell to ring, and a fine piece of work it is. You see, that bell will ring in Palmer's vicarage as long as I shall live, and there is nothing you can do to stop it.'

The story spread and was soon being told in Wilcot. After Cantelow's arrest, Carter kept a low profile and said no more about the matter. If he and Palmer had little to say to each other as Palmer took his solitary dinner in the inn, his haunted eyes staring forward so that he didn't have to look any of his parishioners in the eye, well, Palmer had little to say to anyone anymore.

The story spread all the way to court. Sir George, who'd heard the ringing and shaken his head over it, told the tale to the other lords. In time, even King Charles heard of it. The young King loved masques full of fairies and spirits, but had a horror of such things in real life. Keen for this wild tale to be quashed, he sent a sensible young man to Wilcot to seek the truth of the matter.

When the young man turned up on his doorstep, Palmer was only too grateful to let him in. He was tired of the fear from the villagers who'd heard the bells and the disbelief from those who hadn't. He even had a letter from his bishop telling him to stop his silly tales and get on with his job. As soon the young man stepped inside the house he heard the church bells ring out. He started in wonder.

'It's a ruse, isn't it?' he said to Palmer. 'Some silly jape? You've got some loon over at the church, and a signal so he'll start ringing away as soon as someone enters the house.'

Palmer stared at him. 'You think I do this for my own amusement? If you don't believe me, sir, then I pray you open a window and put your head outside, and tell me what you hear.'

The young man strutted to a window, convinced that he'd hear the bells ringing, but when he opened the glass and leaned out, there was nothing. No sound at all save a blackbird singing in a tree. Quickly, he ducked back into the room, and there were the bells again. He leant out one more time and heard the blackbird, then brought his head back inside to the bells. He stared at Palmer, his face ashen.

'Truly,' he said, 'you have been cursed.'

Nothing could stop the ringing. For year after year the bells rang on in the vicarage. But the very day that Cantlelow died the ringing stopped, never to return again.

This tale comes down to us from Sir George's son, Francis. He passed it on to a certain John Beaumont who included it in his An Historical, Physiological and Theological Treatise of Spirits, Apparitions, Witchcrafts, and Other Magical Practices *of 1705. Beaumont was a doctor and amateur geologist from Ston Easton, near Radstock, in Somerset. He was a learned man, but believed any story he was told and firmly believed that he too had had supernatural experiences: 'some extraordinary visitations having happened to me, in which I have had a converse with those Genii I treat.'*

20

THE FLYING MONK OF MALMESBURY

Five-year-old Eilmer loved the flower meadows near his home. That day, 5 September AD 989, they were thick with the drowsy smell of hay. Eilmer spent as long as he could outside, lying among the late summer flowers and watching the sky. Eilmer watched everything. He loved to watch the ladybirds and the elegant damselflies, but most of all he loved watching birds. More than anything he longed to join them in the branches. He would sweep through the meadow with his arms outstretched, pretending to fly. But that evening he saw something else. Something that would change the course of his life.

It was nearly dark. He knew his mother would worry, but it was warm and pleasant and he loved to watch the stars as well. As the sky darkened he noticed something. Something that hadn't been there the night before. A bright light shone low above the horizon where the sun had set. It was like a tiny sun, a ball of light, but it had a tail streaked out behind it as if it were moving. But it didn't move; it just hung there, bright in the darkness.

Eilmer lay transfixed, not daring to breathe and sure that the next moment would be his last, but unable to take his eyes off the light. In the village he heard screams. But he could only watch the ball of light with its trailing tail. He lay there until he heard his mother calling his name. She sounded close, by the edge of the meadow. With a sigh, Eilmer wrenched his gaze from the light, got up and went to her, bracing himself for her cross words. But she wasn't cross; she dropped to her knees and hugged him tight. He felt tears on his face, and knew that she wept because of the bright light.

Eilmer watched the light over many nights, seeing how, slowly, it moved across the sky until it was gone. He longed to know what he had seen. He pestered his father and the priest until they were at their wits' end. His father hardly knew what to do with all his questions. All the priest could say was that the light made bad things happen. The priest saw that this didn't satisfy the boy and, after a month or so of watching him, came to the father and said, 'He'll never make a farmer. Best give him to the Church.'

Eilmer's father was disappointed, but he had another son and he felt the rightness of the priest's words. Was God not the answer to all questions? So, one day, not so many years later, Eilmer hugged his mother goodbye and set off with his father to walk the long road to the nearest abbey at Malmesbury.

The boy flourished in the care of the Church. He discovered a whole world waiting for him, not just the life of the Church, but knowledge of all of God's creation. Eventually, he found out that what he had seen was a comet. He learnt that Aristotle thought comets the hot and dry exhalations of the upper atmosphere, but that Seneca thought them to be as solid as a piece of rock. He learnt too that they were omens of great events and portents of disaster, and the monks muttered about the Viking raids that still troubled England. Despite this, he longed to see another. The Abbot let him have a room high in the tower of the abbey where he could watch the stars at night.

Aristotle and Seneca were not the only ancient texts the abbey had. Eilmer read everything he could get his hands on, and the Abbot, understanding this need for knowledge, gave him free access to the books. It was in the abbey's library that Eilmer had his second life-changing experience. He took a book from the shelves that had nothing to do with religion and nothing to do with natural science. It was a book of tales from ancient Greece. Among the tales of gods and men, war and women, he found the story of Daedelus.

With rising excitement he read how Daedelus and his son Icarus were trapped on the island of Crete by cruel King Minos, how Daedelus was renowned for his skill in making, and that to escape Minos' clutches Daedelus made wings for himself and his son. Daedelus, Eilmer read, sewed feathers and fixed them together with wax and then he and the boy launched themselves out over the sea and escaped. Eilmer's mind spun. He remembered watching the birds, remembered running, flapping his arms as if they were wings, and he knew what he had to do.

If Eilmer read what happened next – how Daedelus warned his son not to fly too close to the sun in case the wax melted, and how Icarus ignored his father's advice in the sheer joy of flying and plummeted to his death in the unforgiving sea – then it hardly registered in his mind. He would make wings, he would fly, and if he flew high enough he might see Heaven and, perhaps, discover the truth of the comet.

Every day he went out and collected the feathers the wild birds had dropped. He begged feathers from the monk who ran the dovecote and the chicken house. He begged candle ends from the monk who lit the lamps. The Abbot turned a blind eye to the heaps of feathers that piled up in Eilmer's cell.

More than anything, though, Eilmer watched birds. With his own ration of bread he would lay a trail for them. He stayed still and silent, till the birds forgot he was there. It was the jackdaws he watched the most. Chattering, squabbling and flying around him, they showed him how a bird takes off, how it uses its wings, how it lands. The more Eilmer watched, the more he was filled with wonder at God's creation. But the more he watched, the more he realised that he would never be able to fly like a bird.

He was so disappointed he almost gave up. That autumn, though, he watched the ash keys and the sycamore seeds drifting to the ground, and he knew what he could do. Like the seeds, he would catch the wind and let it do the work. He would glide.

All through the winter he made his preparations, until finally the wings were ready. All the monks turned out to watch and a good number of the Malmesbury folk as well. All eyes were turned to the top of the tower.

Eilmer stood on the edge of the tower, the wings strapped to his arms and across his back. A wooden framework supported stretched cloth, like the skin of a sycamore seed, and sewn over that were feathers. Dove white and chicken red and jackdaw black, they glinted resplendently in the sunshine. A breeze ruffled the feathers. Below, the people held their breaths. The Abbot and monks murmured prayers and clacked their rosary beads. Even the birds stopped singing to watch the spectacle.

A gust of wind swept through the abbey grounds and Eilmer stepped out into the empty air. For a moment, he felt the void open beneath him, felt himself dropping with stomach-flipping speed. But then, the wind caught him and he was off.

It was amazing! The rush of the wind around him, the roar of it in his ears, the lift it gave him. He felt as light as a drifting sycamore seed. For a few moments he gloried in pure sensation. Then, above the roar of the wind and the fluttering of the feathers, he heard the cheering of the crowds below, and he did what you should never do when you're up somewhere high.

He looked down.

Down to the pinpricks of people on the ground below. Fear flooded through him. He realised in that moment he was a man held up by nothing but wood, cloth and feathers. He forgot to flap his arms. He forgot to adjust for the wind. He forgot everything he'd learnt from the birds, and he plummeted down.

The cheering stopped. The crowd watched in horror as Eilmer fell through the air towards St Aldhelm's Meadow, just outside the town. He landed with a sickening crash.

The screaming began. Eilmer lay on the ground, the wings broken and smashed around him, his legs twisted in a way that nature never intended. The monks ran to him and began to pray.

But Eilmer was lucky. The meadow was marshy and broke his fall. The monks rushed him to the infirmary, where the infirmarian and his assistants worked all day to straighten his broken legs, set them in bark splints and feed him liquor and herbs when he screamed. The abbey prayed for his soul and that he would find peace serving his Lord, the wings of his soul stretched out proud and fine. They were convinced he would die.

But Eilmer was strong. After a few days of pain and delirium, he awoke with a clear head. The Abbot, sitting beside him, saw his eyes open. He leaned in to catch the man's confession, but Eilmer whispered, 'It would have worked if I'd just had a tail.'

The Abbot banned him from ever trying to fly again.

Eilmer's legs didn't heal as well as he might have hoped, and he often thought of those few moments of flight when his movements had last been free from pain. To feel his limbs floating in air again... But he would never have disobeyed the Abbot. Instead, he went back to watching the night sky. As he grew older he never left his tower room. He lived simply to commune with the stars. The Abbot understood. This was Eilmer's way of worshipping God.

The last year of Eilmer's long life brought one last surprise. On 20 March 1066, when he was eighty-two, he saw something that he hadn't seen since he was five. Watching the sun set, he noticed that, as the sunlight faded from the sky, there was another light still shining. A ball of light with a tail streaming out behind it.

A comet. The comet.

Eilmer was filled at first with the joy he had felt as a boy. But he was no longer a boy. He had learnt many things and knew that the comet meant great change. As he watched the comet his joy was replaced by dread, and with a deepening sense of certainty he knew in his soul what the comet foretold.

'You are come!' he cried. 'You've come, you matter of lamentation to many mothers. It is long since I saw you; but now I behold you are much more terrible, for I see you threatening to hurl destruction on this country.'

Only months later Eilmer died. On 14 October that year William, Duke of Normandy, and King Harold II of England fought on Senlac Hill near Hastings. It is well known what happened that day. William I was like firebrand, spreading war and confusion throughout the land.

Eilmer's prophesy had come true.

William of Malmesbury, writing in the twelfth century, records Eilmer's flight and witnessing of the comet. If Eilmer saw the comet in 1066, it must have been Halley's Comet, which is famously embroidered on the Bayeux Tapestry. Eilmer's flight in around 1010 is one of the first recorded flights in history. Little happened in the development of flight technology between his flight and that of Sir George Cayley, the Yorkshire baronet who designed the first successful gilder in 1799.

21

SQUIRE CROWDY
OF HIGHWORTH

As he was rich, you'd have called Squire Crowdy of Highworth an eccentric. If he hadn't been rich, no doubt he wouldn't have got away with the things he did. Mind you, he punished himself. If he ever did something wrong, Squire Crowdy would take out a halter from his bedroom chest and put it round his neck like a hangman's noose. Then he would walk through the town to demonstrate he'd been wicked. Mostly, the townsfolk tried to ignore it. After all, what could you say? You couldn't have a joke with the Squire, could you? Besides, it was embarrassing. If you said you were from Highworth at the market in Swindon or Faringdon, people would smile. They wouldn't say anything, no. But they'd smile, and that was bad enough. After all, wasn't the Squire just a jumped-up solicitor?

Sometimes, it was difficult to avoid him. He lent his half-peck measure for the grain to a neighbour, and then after waiting a suitable time for it to be returned, decided to take action. He went to the house of the town crier and whispered in his ear, and the very next day the crier was out on the streets, crying, 'Lost! Mr Crowdy lent his half-peck measure to an unknown man. This is to give notice that if the said unknown person doesn't bring it back,

Mr Crowdy will never lend it to him anymore.' The neighbour scuttled round to Crowdy's house pretty sharpish, I can tell you, and never asked to borrow anything from Crowdy again.

Now, Highworth at that time had a wise man who could be relied on to come up with little gems of wisdom, or tell your fortune, or read your dreams for a penny or two, or a dram at the Bull, where he'd tell you about the giant for free. Squire Crowdy was interested in science and modern thinking, and he was quick to dismiss the wise man's words when he heard them bandied about the town. But, in the true spirit of empirical research, he decided that he must put the wise man to the test.

One day, Crowdy encountered the wise man shambling up the street in his stoved-in top hat and his raggedy coat. Crowdy called him over.

'Tell me, my man, what dreams have you been having recently?'

The old man looked Crowdy up and down, and for a long moment he said nothing.

Crowdy began to get angry. 'Come now, man, there should be no secrets here!'

The old man smiled then. He looked Crowdy straight in the eye and said, 'I did have a dream, right enough. Just last night it was.'

By now Crowdy was almost apoplectic with anticipation.

'Well? Come now, man, tell me what it was!' The old man's gaze slid along the High Street to the Bull. Crowdy knew he had met his match. He allowed the wise man to lead him into the pub and procured him a pint. Once settled behind his pint, the old man seemed to relax. Crowdy leaned forward with avid attention.

'I dreamed I was in Hell,' began the old man. Crowdy burst out laughing at this evidence of a superstitious outlook.

'Well now,' he said, 'and what was it like?'

The old man gave him that look again, and again Crowdy felt a prickle of unease and shifted in his seat.

'Those with money,' said the old man, 'they sat nearest to the fire.'

'Is that all?' cried Crowdy.

'Now you mention it,' said the wise man, 'there was a bit more. I was feeling a bit cold – the cold gets into my old bones these days – so up I went to the fire, thinking to warm myself. Right up close to the fire there was the loveliest old chair you've ever seen, all made out of gold. I'm not afraid to tell you that I fancied myself on that chair. So I started to sit down, but as soon as I did there was an almighty shout and a clattering of hooves, and there was the Devil himself standing right in front of me.

"'You mustn't sit there,' he cried.

I was offended. Who was the Devil to be a-telling me what to do? "And why not?" I asked.

The Devil gave me a fierce look and replied, "Because that's reserved for old Crowdy of Highworth!"'

Squire Crowdy laughed it off as a joke and never troubled the wise man again. But laughing about Hell is easy enough when you are a young man full of the vigour of life. As Crowdy grew older, and his breath grew short in his chest, he found that the old certainties of his youth faded and his mind kept going back to that day, dwelling on the wise man's words.

Then, one day as he was sitting in his study, reading quietly and nursing his customary glass of port, he felt a sudden sharp pain in his chest. The glass fell to the floor and Crowdy fell back in his seat. When he opened his eyes he saw a figure standing in front of him. A figure wearing a long black hooded cloak, grinning at him. Not that the figure had any choice but to grin: its face was a skull.

Squire Crowdy knew exactly who this was. Clutching his chest, he cried, 'No, I shan't die!'

Death looked at him long and hard, then said, 'Too late.'

Crowdy leapt out of his chair to push Death away, but when he looked around again he saw himself slumped in his seat and he knew that what Death had said was true. But, though he was dead, he realised that he was still himself.

'I shan't go with you!' he cried. 'Not with that golden chair waiting for me!'

Now, Death had heard it all before, what with the likes of Squire Wareford over at South Marston not fifty years back, who'd said he wasn't giving up hunting yet and had ridden off into the night with his ghostly hounds. Death could wait. Everyone came to him in the end. He grinned at Crowdy and then faded away.

Squire Crowdy flexed his ghostly muscles. Now he thought about it, he felt great. Better than he had done for years. Looking down at himself, he realised he looked better than he had done for years as well. He grinned. He could have some fun with this. There'd been little enough fun these last few years. He went upstairs to his bedroom and opened the chest at the foot of the bed. Well, at least a ghostly lid came up. Nestled in the bottom of the chest was a ghostly halter. He reached in and put it round his neck.

At first he wasn't too ambitious, just walked up and down Cricklade Road and the High Street with the halter on as he had done in his youth. Not many people were out after dark, so he found it more effective if he howled a bit. People would run then and maybe scream and bang their shutters closed.

It was great fun. He even took himself to South Marston once and went hunting with old Wareford, singing out a ghostly 'Tally-ho!' But after a while he tired of these soft measures and decided to raise the stakes. He picked up the shafts of his own coach and drew it out along his drive and onto Cricklade Street and clattered it up and down to strike terror into the citizens of Highworth.

Such fun!

Except that people now stayed in more, so there were fewer people to scare.

The people of Highworth were at their wits' end. Every night, it seemed, the ghost would do something to terrify them. There was nothing they could do to stop it. It went on and on, year after year, until at last the townsfolk decided they could put up with it no longer. A body of men got together to lay the ghost and send him to his eternal rest.

The Vicar, the bailiff and the jurymen set out one dark night to Westrop House, deserted since the haunting began. They arranged themselves in a circle, lit their candles and started to call the spirit. Terror flickered the candles in their hands.

When Crowdy first felt the pull of their prayers, he was intrigued, but then he realised what was going on and tried to resist. But the pull of the prayers was too great and he found himself in the middle of their circle.

'You'll not take me,' he cried. 'I'll never submit to the golden chair!'

That meant nothing to the townsfolk.

The Vicar stepped forward and said, 'Come now, Squire Crowdy. Ever since I came to this parish I've heard about you scaring the town, but I've heard too that when you were alive you were a good and fair squire, who had the best interests of the town at heart, despite all your joking. Surely you can't think that scaring the people of your town out of their wits is the best thing for them?'

Crowdy opened his mouth to protest. Then he thought about it, and he hung his head.

'Very well,' he said. 'I'll go, but on one condition: that you lay me to rest in one of the barrels of fine cider that are still in my cellar, for if I'm going to go to Hell I'd rather go happy than sad.'

He led them down to his cellar and, sure enough, several barrels of cider were sitting in the dust.

Gingerly, the Vicar stepped forward and pulled out the bung from one of them. Crowdy jumped in. The Vicar smacked the bung in again as fast as he could, and called for someone to run for the mason and his lads.

The mason came hurrying over with his apprentices and they bricked up the cellar. After that, the people of Highworth were able to rest easy in their beds, for Squire Crowdy was never seen again. But what of the golden chair? Is Squire Crowdy nestled up against the fire in Hell? Well, it's been a good many years now, so I reckon that cider's all drunk – so if any of you end up down there in Hell, why don't you go and see if you can find him?

The stories of Squire Crowdy were collected by Alfred Williams in Round About the Upper Thames. *Squire Crowdy was a real man. He was probably William Crowdy, a solicitor who bought the Manor, Borough and Hundred of Highworth in 1806 and built Westrop House about ten years later. He died in 1838 – just long enough before Williams was collecting for any eccentricities to have become legend.*

22

THE LEGEND OF
THE WHITE HAND

John Long wasn't the sharpest knife in the box, but everyone said he was an amiable young man. A little too fond of gambling, perhaps, and the cause of a headache or two to his father, Walter, but a more generous and easygoing young man was hard to find. His mother died when he was young, and he was his father's only child. He grew up in the comfortable knowledge that his father's estates at Draycot Cerne and South Wraxall would one day be his.

However, his father had other ideas. He decided to marry again, into the illustrious line of the Thynnes of Longleat. It was a good match, better than his first. By rights, young John should have been worried and maybe have changed his ways. Walter watched him carefully on the wedding day, but his son seemed his usual affable self, quite unconcerned.

Six weeks later Walter and his new bride, Catherine, arrived at Draycot House. For a few minutes John was silent as his father led his wife to her place at the head of the table. He dimly remembered his mother sitting there, but his warm nature soon won through. He raised the first toast to his father and wished the happy couple joy for the future. Catherine looked into her new son's open face with sharp eyes, and after a long moment she smiled.

The young bride was more of an age to the son than the father, and John was a pleasant-looking young man. But Catherine was a sharp one and not likely to make a costly mistake. She studied John closely. She saw how he would sit in the hall with his friends for hours as the cards were cut and the money moved about. She saw how those so-called friends would come to him at quiet moments and how he would give them money, which he never saw again. She saw too how her husband frowned at his son's bills, and emptied his pockets with a weary sigh. At first she did nothing. But when after a few months of marriage she felt life stirring in her, her way became clear.

First she sent for her brother, Sir Egremont Thynne. This young man was as canny as his sister. He understood the situation instantly.

'This wastrel,' said Catherine, 'must not fritter away my child's inheritance!'

It was clear to them that Catherine's child must inherit it all. John Long must be ruined, disgraced and beggared. And it would be all too easy to do.

Sir Egremont sent for his friends from Longleat, and they soon settled into life of Draycot House. With their easy manners and free spending at the gaming tables, they soon became John's friends. If John's money ran dry, his new friends would laugh and press gold into his hands. Of course, John did the same for them. In town, they would hustle him to the tailor's or the bootmaker's or the horses and encourage him to spend. John never noticed that his new friends placed only the smallest of bets. He only heard their sweet words and saw sincere friendship in their eyes.

But when he wasn't there, his new friends would talk of John's excesses and soberly shake their heads and sigh.

'That boy, if he's not checked, he'll go to the bad.'

''Tis such a shame to see a great manor like this ruined. I fear that if young John continues the way he does...'

'Have you heard? He spent £50 just on a pair of riding boots!'

Sir Walter listened to all this, and to Sir Egremont's sober reports. He was not surprised. 'The boy was spoilt after his mother died. I left him too long with his nurses. I should have taken a firmer hand.'

His wife said little, but in private would express concern about her own baby's future should the young heir continue in this way. When the babe was born a strong and healthy boy, it was easy to see the father's mind working. This son could be moulded into a serious, sensible man. This one would be the son of his dreams. And the other son? Well, in truth, Sir Walter thought of John less and less.

The baby was not yet a year old when Sir Walter sickened. Catherine couldn't have been a more devoted carer and was always at his bedside. But still he faded. The brother and sister knew they had to act fast. Sir Egremont drew up a new will and pressed the sick man to sign. It cut John out of all his inheritance and implicated him in shameful deeds. Once signed, everything would go to the baby. Sir Walter signed without any need for coercion. As soon as Sir Walter gave permission for the document to be copied, Sir Egremont brought Sir Walter's old engrossing clerk to copy it out in a fair hand. The old man had written out documents for the family for many years, even the marriage contract between Sir Walter and his first wife.

The clerk was put in a bright room in Draycot House. Copying needs good light to ensure that no mistake is made that might invalidate the document. Then as now, wills tended to be long and involved documents. The clerk soon fell into a trancelike state of not really reading what he wrote, but of making sure that what he wrote matched what was written. It was midday when he started, and the light clear and good, so he was startled when a shadow fell across the page.

He looked up, thinking someone had come into the room. There was no one there, but the cause of the shadow was plain to see. A ghostly white hand, small and womanly, seemed to float across the parchment, obscuring the next thing he was to write. The clerk frowned, blinked, then shook his head and rubbed his eyes.

'Time for a break,' he muttered, and stretched in his seat. When he looked back again, the hand was gone. He laughed that he had imagined such a thing, and scanned the text before of him. The elder son, he read, was to be disinherited. The clerk frowned.

He remembered the boy's mother well, and felt a moment of sadness that young John was to be cut out of the will. But it wasn't for him to say. He picked up his pen, dipped it in the ink and then leaned over the parchment again.

But as soon as he looked back at the page, the white hand was there again, blocking his view. For a moment the clerk stared, mesmerised, as the hand drifted over the parchment. It was no trick of the light. It was real, and he knew what it must be. He shoved back his stool and ran straight to Sir Egremont.

'The hand!' he cried. 'Lady Long has returned from the next world! She's protecting her son!' The clerk refused to carry on and left, swearing never to set foot in Draycot House again.

Sir Egremont was shaken, but he refused to give in. Swiftly, before rumour put paid to his work, he hired another clerk. This one was able to copy the document without any problems. This clerk didn't care what these rich men did with their heirs so long as his own bill was paid.

Sir Walter obligingly died soon after, and his baby son inherited his entire estate.

John Long was devastated, but he found that his good nature had won him true friends. The first clerk had spread the story of the ghostly white hand far and wide, and friends and relatives of John's mother rallied to him. On the day of his father's funeral, his late mother's trustees marched up behind the coffin and stopped it entering the church.

'By the powers invested in me,' cried one, 'I arrest you, Sir Walter Long of Draycot Cerne and South Wraxall!'

They took out a lawsuit against the dead knight and his baby son to contest the will. In the end a compromise was reached. Baby Walter took Draycot House and John inherited South Wraxall. It is not recorded if the young man learnt the error of his ways but, whether he did or not, he must have remembered his debt to his mother for the rest of his days.

This story is recorded in John Timbs's Abbeys, Castles and Ancient Halls *as coming from J. Bernard Burke's* Anecdotes of the Aristocracy *of 1849, although the story takes places in the early seventeenth century. Burke was the son of John Burke of Burke's Peerage.* Anecdotes *was a rather more salacious and popular version of the father's serious tome.*

23

FLYING WILL CONTINUE AS USUAL

Captain Eustace Loraine laughed out loud, feeling the rush of the wind against his bare pink cheeks. His face was the only part of him not swaddled against the cold. Ever since his first flight, the year before in 1911, he had been filled with joy each time he had taken to the air. He grinned over his shoulder at Wilson, his staff sergeant, who smiled back and gave him the thumbs up. What larks at Larkhill! In the late afternoon sunshine, Loraine eased the little Neiuport IV-G Monoplane a touch higher and swung around over the airfield. The men below scurried across the field like ants as they went about their business. Loraine felt on top of the world. He cruised out over Stonehenge for the second time that day. This, he was sure, was what he had been born to do.

Loraine was in No. 3 Squadron of the newly formed Royal Flying Corps. He'd joined up as fast as he could after hearing about Louis Blériot's flight across the Channel. He was in the air every day. He didn't care about the weather or the way these small machines of wood and canvas fell apart all the time. Like earlier today: the Nieuport had slipped during a left turn and misfired. They'd been lucky to get back in one piece.

Wilson agreed with him that it had been a miserable week, especially for July. He was a useful man with an engine and just as keen to be in the air as Loraine. Promising fellow, thought Loraine, for all Wilson was just an NCO and a grammar-school boy. The week had been beastly, with rain and fog and that blasted wind that never stopped blowing across the Plain.

Loraine dipped the plane low over the ancient stones, close enough to see the green and grey smears of lichen on their tops. Then he took the plane up to 350 feet and swung away to the east over Fargo Bottom.

'Going to turn her around, sharp,' he shouted back at Wilson. 'See if she's still playing up.'

That was the last time anyone saw Loriane and Wilson alive.

Sir Michael Bruce, baronet, did not consider himself a man of nervous disposition. Denied a career in the forces by his father's debts and early death, he had joined the British South African Police. He had killed an escaped criminal before his eighteenth birthday and captured a double murderer before his nineteenth. The First World War had made a soldier of him, at last, but he was invalided out of the forces straight after the war. He sought adventure in South America – took part in a revolution in Brazil, climbed the Andes, and was the only survivor of an expedition seeking treasure in the Amazon. In the 1930s he settled down with his wife, Constance, and wrote for magazines, but the prospect of a new war stirred his blood.

At first he stayed in Vienna, arranging the escape of Jews. This dangerous life couldn't last, however, and he was soon in danger of being caught by the Germans. He made his way home. This time he decided to indulge his desire to fly. With great excitement, Bruce joined Sir Kingsley Wood's 'Old Man's Battalion' flying barrage balloons. But this only lasted a few months and Bruce ended up writing propaganda films.

Eventually he managed to persuade the authorities that he would be more use to his country in uniform than behind a desk, and he got clearance to fly again. But his enthusiasm for the war soon waned. Tragedy struck. His beloved Constance died after a bomb landed on their Hertfordshire home. Shortly before D-Day, though, he was given a new assignment, and sent on a training exercise at RAF Larkhill.

Bruce might have attributed what he saw that day to his grief at losing his wife, still fresh after one year, if it hadn't been that the other men in his party saw exactly the same thing.

He and three other trainees were travelling up the road from Salisbury with an RAF warrant officer to look for spots to position guns in the next day's training exercise. The four of them were laughing and joking with each other in the back of the jeep while the warrant officer concentrated on steering through the roaring wind.

'It's always like this up here,' he shouted over the din. 'Bloody desolate place for practice!'

It was so windy that they didn't hear anything else at first, but after a while Bruce's ears picked up a thin chuntering above the wind, then the sputtering sound of an engine misfiring.

'What's that?' he cried. The warrant officer halted the jeep, and they all looked up. Above the line of trees along the road they saw a little plane silhouetted against the late afternoon sky.

'That's strange,' said the warrant officer. 'Looks like an old Neiuport IV-G. Not many of them around.'

'Need every plane available, don't we?' said one of the recruits. 'Need 'em all against the Hun.'

As they watched, the little plane twisted to the left as if in a fancy turn, but then dropped, tumbling down, down, spinning in the harsh wind until it disappeared behind the trees. For a moment the five men sat frozen in place. Then the warrant officer sped the jeep towards the T-junction. There was no sign of smoke or fire. The men clambered up the bank, then spread out and searched behind the trees. The field beyond was empty of any sign of a crash. They scanned the sky to see if they could spot the little plane flying safely away, but the grey sky was empty.

'Must've gone behind a cloud,' muttered Bruce as he climbed back down to the jeep again.

Then, he heard a shout from the warrant officer.

Bruce turned and ran back. The warrant officer stood at the junction, his face as white as a sheet. In front of him, in an island of grass, stood a lichen-crusted stone cross. Bruce frowned. He must have been along this road a hundred times, yet he'd never noticed it.

He went and stood next to the warrant officer and read the inscription. A shudder ran through him.

> To the Memory of Captain Loraine and Staff Sergeant Wilson who whilst flying on duty met with a fatal accident near this spot July 5th 1912. Erected by their comrades.

Bruce knew then they would never find anything associated with the crash they'd seen. No plane, no bodies. The bodies were long gone. Bruce stared at the stone cross and wondered who Loraine and Wilson were; wondered if they too had felt the same thrill in flying that he did, and wondered too how they had felt as their little plane crashed to the ground. He closed his eyes and thought of his own lost wife, dead because of the actions of an aeroplane in this hellish war.

Then the warrant officer clapped him on the back and the two of them headed back to the jeep where the others were already waiting. They had work to do. Flying would continue as usual.

Captain Eustace Loraine, thirty-three, and Staff Sergeant Richard Wilson, twenty-nine, were the first members of the Royal Flying Corps, which later became the RAF, to die while on duty. Their comrades were watching from the airfield at Larkhill and raced off immediately in a car to try to save them. Wilson was killed immediately upon impact, and Loraine died from his injuries soon after arriving at the hospital at Bulford. The memorial cross, still rather covered in lichen, can be seen as you come up the A360 towards Stonehenge. A new plaque added in 1996 tells the story. It was Bruce who alerted the world to his ghostly sighting of the plane in 1944, by writing a letter to the Evening Standard *nine years later in 1953.*

24

THE MAID AND
THE MAGGOT

One fine morning in the month of September, a young girl went nutting in Grovelly Wood. She gathered sweet chestnuts and walnuts, beechnuts and acorns; but her favourites were hazelnuts. She cracked them there and then and stuffed them in her mouth as fast as she picked them.

Then, just as she was about to pop another tasty morsel into her mouth she noticed something. Sitting inside the shell was a fat, shiny maggot. The girl opened her mouth to scream, but then she looked again. The maggot was quite appealing, with its shiny white segments, and its little pointy black face looking up at her. It reminded her of her father's black-faced sheep.

'I think I'll take you home.' Very carefully, she balanced the nut on top of the others in the basket and set off home to Little Langford. There she found a little wooden box and filled it up with sheep's wool from her mother's spinning bag. Gently she laid the maggot inside.

'Now,' she said, 'I wonder what you eat.' First she played safe and fed the maggot some of the nuts she'd collected that day. It soon grew as big as a bee.

But the girl didn't stop. She fed it cheese, and soon the maggot was the size of a mouse. She fed it fresh fish from the river, and it grew until it was the size of a cat. She would sit by the fire with it on her lap and stroke its shiny white skin, so taut and warm, and tickle it under its pointy black chin.

Her parents started to get a little worried. 'Are you sure you know what you're doing, dear?' asked her mother.

'Of course I do,' she said. But she didn't stop there. She fed the maggot old bones and it grew to be the size of a dog, and a big one at that. It took to following her around wherever she went, and it would growl if her parents came near. But she didn't notice, she loved it so dearly.

But she didn't stop there. She fed it scraps and old roots, and it grew to be the size of a pig, its taut shiny skin tight almost to bursting. It grew so big that it couldn't come in the house anymore. She had to keep it outside in the spare pigsty. The girl would hang over the gate and coochicoo it all day long if she could get away with it.

But she didn't stop there. The maggot was so big that it was getting hard to feed. All that was left was grass, so she fed it that, and it grew to be the size of a cow.

At that point the maggot took charge. It ripped the door off its shed, and ate it. It ate the trough, it ate the straw. It ate the bricks and it ate the floor, and it made such a racket that the maid came running out to see what was up with her pet.

The maggot looked her up and down.

Then it bit the hand that fed it.

But it didn't stop there. It ate the maid up until there was nothing left but her shoes.

After that, there was no stopping it. It ate the pigs, it ate the sheep. It ate the chickens and it hoovered up the vegetables from the vegetable plot, and when the garden was empty, it turned towards the house.

Quick as a flash, it broke down the door, and it crashed about all over the floor. It ate the table and it ate the chairs; it ate the dog hiding under the stairs. It ate the linen and it ate the fat; it ate the ham for supper, and it ate the cat. It ate the beds and it ate the

bath, and it sucked up the dust from all around the hearth. It ate
the fresh meat and it ate the dried, and it ate all the food that had
been put to one side. It ate the curtains and it ate the stairs; it ate
the shoes up in their pairs. It ate the dresses and it ate the socks,
and it even ate the chamber pots.

And when it had finished eating everything inside, it ate the
house as well.

Then it turned towards the village, and it ate the sheep and the
goats and the cows in the fields. By now, it was the size of a house
and getting bigger all the time. The ground shook as it moved. The
villagers heard it before they saw it. They ran screaming from their
houses as it came down the street, scattering horses and carts and
munching them as it went.

The villagers could do nothing but stand and stare as it ate
their houses. It ate the inn, the mill and the forge. Then it headed
towards the church. The villagers knew they had to act. They
couldn't let it take the house of God. So they gathered up all the
sticks and stones they could find and ran after it. They pelted it
until it howled with rage and turned back, intent on eating them
all. But they kept on beating at it, and just before it reached the

church it turned and headed off back into Grovelly Wood, from whence it had come.

The villagers followed the maggot and tracked through the wide avenues of trees. But it was as if it had vanished into thin air. And by now it was nearly night, and no one wanted to face it in there after dark. There was only one thing to be done: to tell the Lord of the Manor. The Lord of the Manor listened, and then ordered his finest archers and hunters to go into Grovelly Wood at first light and put an end to the beast.

The next morning the lord's men went armed with sticks, spears, bows and arrows. They spread out to make a cordon and searched the wood. But they couldn't find the maggot. The villagers had said it was as big as a house. Surely such a large beast couldn't hide? They asked themselves, 'Have the villagers played a trick on us?'

They decided to head back to the village when someone shouted.

They all spun around.

There, right in front of them, was the biggest, the most horrible, white gleaming thing. As big as a house it was, all wrapped around and around with shiny white threads. But it wasn't the maggot.

One of the hunters dared to approach with his spear held high. When he reached the thing, he leaned in as close as he dared, then reached out with his spear, and prodded it with its tip.

There was a bang, and the thing exploded. Silk and slime flew everywhere.

The hunters flung themselves to the ground and covered their heads. When they at last dared to look up, they stared around in puzzlement. There was nothing to be seen. Yes, there was the odd bit of silk and the odd bit of slime, but hardly enough to account for a beast of that size.

The hunters shrugged their shoulders and went home, congratulating themselves on killing the beast. What else could they do? They'd killed something. But if only they'd thought to look up through the trees to the sky, they'd have seen something that would have made them scream and run till they were safe inside.

There, high up in the sky, spiralling round and round as it rode the thermals in the air, was a freshly hatched young dragon. If they had watched, they would have seen it heading west – to Somerset, where such beasts are common.

This story is based on the tympanum over the door of Little Langford Church. The picture is thought to represent St Aldhelm and his miraculous ash tree, but that's not how the villagers saw it. To them, the tympanum depicted a figure in a dress with its hands upraised, standing next to a tree. Above and around that is a semi-circle of jagged decoration that looks a lot like teeth. Villagers say that the figure is the maid and the teeth are those of the maggot. The picture, they say, shows the maid being eaten up by the beast. Carved in the stone below that is a hunting scene, and the villagers say that shows the beast being rounded up by the hunters. The story echoes many tales of unsuspecting people nurturing something that turns out to be a dragon – or, as they are often called in England, a worm. Now, worms and maggots, it could be argued, are fairly similar in looks, so I suggest that the maggot is really a dragon. Dragon stories are very rare in Wiltshire, but in Somerset there are many.

25

ST MELOR OF THE SILVER HAND

The kingdoms of Britain and Brittany shared an ancient bond of friendship. When the Romans left Britain and France to fight the invaders at home, the bond had never been needed more. As the kingdoms of Britain collapsed and fought amongst themselves, it was King Budic I of Cornouaille, in south-west Brittany, who offered the hand of friendship to the young brothers of murdered King Constans.

Ambrosius Aurelianus and his brother Uther Pendragon grew up alongside Budic's own sons, Meliau and Riwal. Perhaps through the tragedy they had shared, Ambrosius and Uther loved each other well, but there was little love lost between Budic's sons. Meliau was a popular boy, handsome and easygoing. Riwal resented everything his brother did. Now, Budic was a wise and well-respected leader, but his sons were his one blind spot. He didn't – or wouldn't – see how Meliau ignored his brother and how Riwal grew to hate Meliau. But in his heart he must have sensed something was wrong. He saw there was a shadow on Riwal.

In those days it was not the custom to leave the kingdom to the first-born son, but to give it to the most worthy. Budic looked at his sons, and he decided to leave everything to Meliau. He didn't leave Riwal a single manor house.

Budic kept this to himself until his dying day. As Riwal listened to his father's dying words, he burned with anger. As soon as his father was dead, he went to his brother and demanded he reconsider their father's judgement.

'He must have been mad! Brother, it would be honourable to divide the kingdom with me. It cannot have been our father's wish to see me starve!'

Meliau looked at Riwal in surprise. His brother couldn't mean it, could he? Riwal rule? It was out of the question, and he told him so.

Riwal argued and wheedled and begged, but it was no good. Meliau gave him a place in his war band, but on the issue of land he wouldn't give way, and as time went on their resentment came spilling out in hurtful words. Riwal was feckless and cruel and cared nothing for the land. Meliau was spoilt and uncaring and didn't respect his family. They could not meet without exchanging harsh words.

'You should send him into exile,' counselled Meliau's nobles. 'Root out the weed before it spoils the crop.'

But this was his brother, and in his heart Meliau knew that his brother had been wronged. But he knew too that to offer him a manor would give him the toehold he needed. Riwal would never let up his fight to rule. Meliau feared war and he hesitated, uncertain of what to do.

While Meliau dithered, Riwal came to his brother and they argued again, shouting and screaming at each other. Riwal grew angrier and angrier, and Meliau wouldn't give an inch. Riwal's sword found its way into his hand and, without thinking, he reached out and thrust it into his brother's heart. Meliau fell down dead at his feet.

Whether the murder was planned or not, Riwal acted fast. He seized the castle and married the widowed Queen. The nobles dared not make any objection, and he was crowned King. But there was a problem. Meliau had a son, Melor, a boy of seven years.

There were murmurings in the court that the boy was the rightful King, and Riwal knew he had to be dealt with. The boy had to die.

'Please don't kill the child,' his nobles begged. 'It will stain your soul to kill such an innocent. Send him away, foster him with Uther Pendragon in Britain, and all will be well.'

Riwal knew that the innocent would grow to be a threat in a few short years, and that sending him to be trained as a warrior in Britain would only make it worse. But he didn't wish to antagonise his nobles at this precarious time. They could turn on him at any second, he knew, so instead he ordered that the child be maimed.

No man could rule Cornouaille if he couldn't wield a sword or ride a horse. So, Riwal ordered that the boy have his right hand and his left foot chopped off. He hoped in his secret heart that Melor might die from the shock. But the boy survived and, worse, the nobles pitied him. They made a silver hand and a bronze foot for the boy. Riwal soon made it clear that Melor was not safe at court. One of his nobles, Cerialtan, spirited the boy away in the night and took him to the school at Quimper Abbey.

Safely within the walls of the abbey, the frightened boy began to settle. He made friends among the boys who studied there, and enjoyed his lessons. If he was sad when he watched his friends running and practising swordplay and archery, he said nothing. No one breathed a word that he was there. He was safe.

But then, Melor began to feel something strange. It was as if he had his missing foot and hand again, tingling, itching. He tried to ignore it. An old warrior had told him this might happen, that missing limbs can itch and feel pain years after they were lost. But the feeling wouldn't go away, and one day as he sat at his lessons one of his silver fingers moved. With growing excitement and wonder he flexed his silver fingers and bent his bronze toes. They worked just as his foot and hand had done before.

It was a miracle. Everyone was sworn to secrecy at the abbey. Melor grew as boys do, and his metal limbs grew with him. But, of course, he wasn't quite like the other boys. Once, when he was out collecting nuts with his friends near the abbey gate, he threw away some nutshells and, in doing so, he bashed his metal hand against the gate. His hand passed through the gate as if it was nothing but air. Another time, practising his bowmanship, he missed his shot and the arrow plunged deep into a stone and from that spot a spring burst from the rock.

These things couldn't be hidden. The rumours began to spread.

It didn't take long before the news came to Riwal that the boy could ride and fight as well as any boy his age. God had touched him, the rumour ran. The whispers at court began to grow.

'Melor is the rightful King,' they said. 'God has shown his approval. He wants Melor to rule.'

Riwal had to silence the whispers. There was only one way. The death of a fourteen-year-old young man was far less shocking than that of a boy of seven, wasn't it?

Riwal visited Melor's guardian Cerialtan at Quimper. Cerialtan realised that Melor's cover was blown, and he feared for his own life. When the King ordered him to accompany him up Mount Frugy just outside the city, he had no choice but to obey. From Mount Frugy you could see the whole of the city and the farm-lands beyond.

Riwal gestured to the view and said, 'Kill Melor and bring me his head, and all the land you can see from the top of this hill will be yours.'

Cerialtan was horrified. How could he kill the boy who was his ward and the best friend of his own son, Justan? But the King's words stayed with him. He confided in his wife, but she didn't respond in the way he expected.

'All of Quimper is visible from Mount Frugy,' she said. 'Think what good you would be doing for your own son! You have to do it. You know Melor is doomed. Riwal will kill him one way or another, so you might as well be the one who gets the reward.'

Cerialtan bowed his head. 'Very well,' he said.

But later that day Cerialtan's wife watched her boy and Melor playing football in the courtyard together, and she knew she had spoken in haste and greed. So she went to Melor and told him that the two of them must flee. Melor wasn't stupid, he had understood the danger he was in for many years, but it was hard from him to believe that the threat came from his own guardian. But he knew he could take no chances. He agreed to go. They fled across the border to the kingdom of East Cornouaille, where King Poher ruled.

When Riwal heard the news, he was furious.

'Get that boy's head and bring it to me,' he told Cerialtan. 'I swear a head is going to roll. If you don't bring me Melor's head, I'll have Justan's instead.'

Cerialtan had no choice. Dragging Justan with him, he went to Poher's castle and begged admittance. 'For who can separate a man from his wife?'

Poher let him in and Cerialtan went to his wife, but he didn't tell her what Riwal had told him. His wife pleaded with him for Melor's life, and Cerialtan agreed. He watched grimly as the two boys were reunited, and that night he ensured they were placed together in one chamber. If Melor was uneasy, he didn't dare say anything. He saw that Cerialtan's wife was powerless now her husband was here. That night as he went to bed, he said his prayers with great passion and then he lay there trying desperately to keep awake.

Later, Cerialtan crept into the room. He found both boys fast asleep. He stared for a long time at his own sleeping son. Then he went to Melor. He didn't allow himself to hesitate. He raised his sword and with one stroke he struck off Melor's head.

He stuffed the head into a sack then shook his son awake. The boy awoke to a room soaked in blood, his best friend dead and his father the murderer. In deep shock, he followed his father. As they fled through the castle, Cerialtan watched him. The boy was silent, but he seemed calm. The gates were locked, so they had to climb the walls. As they scaled the walls to freedom, Cerialtan allowed himself to think that all would be well. But just as they reached the top Justan turned to look at him, and lost his footing. Cerialtan lunged for him, but it was too late. The boy crashed to the hard ground below.

For a few desperate minutes Cerialtan watched his son's body, willing it to rise. It was no good. His son was dead. When he heard sounds of the guards approaching he forced himself on, the tears streaking his face not only for his son but for the ruin of all his life. For hours there was nothing but a grim placing of one foot in front of the other. But at last he reached the end of his strength and collapsed on a bleak hill, desperate with grief and thirst.

As he lay there on the grass, his breath coming in ragged bursts, he heard a voice from the sack that held Melor's head. It was a voice he had heard many times before, laughing with his son. A light, high young voice. Melor's voice.

'Cerialtan, listen to me.'

And Cerialtan listened. 'Strike your staff into the soil and water will spring up.'

Cerialtan was filled with fear but he dared not disobey the ghostly voice. He plunged his staff into the earth and, as he watched, a spring gushed forth and his staff blossomed into a living tree. He did not stop to marvel, but fell to his knees and drank.

He hardly knew what to do next. The head had spoken. A miracle had taken place. But Cerialtan felt that he might as well get the land he had lost so much for, so he picked up the sack and continued on his way to Riwal's court. He presented his prize to the King. When Riwal took the head and held it aloft in triumph, Cerialtan said nothing of the miracle or his own son's death.

The next day, with a heart of lead, Cerialtan returned to Quimper. There, son-less and with his wife still gone, he trudged up Mount Frugy to view his hollow reward. But when he reached the top and looked out over his new land, he was struck blind.

People spoke of a curse and it seemed they were right, for just three days after news of Cerialtan's blindness came to the court, Riwal himself dropped down dead.

Riwal's uncle Erich took the throne and immediately called for an honourable burial for Melor. The boy's head was reunited with his body, but his spirit did not rest easy in the grave. Every day they buried him and every night they found Melor's body up on the ground in the morning. The people despaired that the curse would ever be lifted. But one day two untamed bulls turned up at the graveside and allowed a cart to be hitched to their shoulders. They pulled Melor's body to Lanmeur, where a church was founded in his honour.

Over the years there were many miracles at the church. Melor was made a saint and for a long time all was well. But many years later, Melor's rest was threatened. When the Normans came, war raged throughout France and the monks of Brittany gathered up their holy relics and fled across the sea to England to seek safety in Wessex, recently secured against the Vikings by King Alfred the Great.

St Melor's monks fled through Cornwall, up through Devon, across Somerset, not knowing what they should do with the saint. Eventually they were welcomed into the nunnery at Amesbury, which Ambrosius Aurelianus had founded and where Queen Guinevere had died. The relics of the saint were placed on the high altar and a mass of thanksgiving was held in his honour.

But when the monks came to take the relics away they couldn't lift them from the altar. They were stuck fast and nothing anyone could do would lift them away. It was very embarrassing and the monks were furious, and had to be offered a lot of money to go away. St Melor had chosen his new home.

The church was re-consecrated in his name, and for many years people flocked to his healing shrine. St Melor was so popular that Amesbury grew rich on his name. The bones were placed in a golden reliquary encrusted with jewels and enamelled scenes of his life, and the nuns lived well on the saint's fame.

Such an expensive item didn't only attract pilgrims, however. Late one night, many years after the shrine was built, thieves crept into the church. They stole past the altar, grabbed the reliquary and ran. When the nuns came the next morning to worship at the shrine, they found it empty, the only thing left a sheared piece of metal where the thieves had cut the reliquary from the altar. They were horrified. With only days to go before the saint's feast, when thousands would turn up hoping for a miracle, it was a disaster.

Everyone was set to searching, even guests. The town was turned upside down. Everyone from the Abbess to the innkeeper and the baker fell into a panic as they imagined ruin and riots. One guest, though, a monk from the north called Godric of Finchale, went into the woods by the abbey to search.

Godric, they say, was a friend to the animals, who let snakes sleep by his hearth and hid stags from hunters, so it may be that he had help. He made his way through the deserted woods and came to a small cave. He crept inside and, there, tucked behind a stone, was a pile of bones. The reliquary with all its fine gold and jewels was long gone, but he guessed what he had found. He tenderly gathered up the fragile bones and carried them back to the abbey church.

He wanted to find someone to tell them the good news, but as soon as he left the church he saw a young man with a silver hand and a bronze foot standing under the shade of a great yew tree. Godric fell to his knees.

'Do not go, Godric,' cried the saint. 'Go back inside and fetch me out – else I will be lost forever.'

Godric was puzzled but he dared not question or disobey the saint, so he hurried back inside the church and gathered up the remains. No sooner had he left the church he felt a tremor run through him. Instinct told him to run. With the bones clutched tight in his arms, he fled. Only when he reached the abbey walls did he dare to look around. As he turned, he saw the great tower fall and the church collapsed in on itself. The place where the altar had been was utterly destroyed. Godric fell down on his knees and praised God for the miracle, and his own escape thanks to the saint – for in the very place where he had been standing outside the church, there now lay a huge chunk of fallen stone.

With the church in ruins and the bones of the saint gone, the healing shrine could no longer function. Not so long afterwards King Henry II dissolved the abbey and had it rebuilt as a priory under the Order of Fontevrault. But what happened to Melor? It is not known if Godric spirited the bones away, perhaps on Melor's instructions. Godric lived out the rest of his life in his hermitage in Finchale, near Durham, and didn't say a word about where he had hidden the bones. To this day no one knows where the bones lie. Melor was lost for ever..

St Melor has three churches dedicated to him in England. There are two in Cornwall, and he is still remembered at the old abbey church at Amesbury. The abbey in the story was founded in the tenth century by Queen Aelfthrith, the wife of King Edgar. William of Malmesbury says that Aelfthrith was involved in the murder of her stepson St Edward the Martyr. It has been suggested that she chose the spot to atone for her sins as Amesbury already had a shrine to another young murdered Prince, Melor. It is quite possible that the relics of the saint did come to Amesbury in the tenth century as many Bretons fled to Britain when the Normans invaded Brittany.

26

The Black Dog of Collingbourne Kingston

The Bath road wasn't safe at night. Robbers roamed the highway from dusk into the small hours of the night. No carriage was safe. Jewels and fat purses were taken, and sometimes, if the mark fought back, a body would be dragged into the woods, stripped of its clothing and left under a thin shroud of earth. But the people of the Collingbournes and Everleigh turned a blind eye to these goings-on. What did they care that some toffs had lost their fancies or that some rich fool had come a cropper travelling the highway after dark? So long as they and theirs weren't troubled, then such things were best left alone.

But that winter was hard and precious few people were making any kind of journey, let alone after dark when the temperatures dropped below freezing and could easily kill. With no easy pickings on the road, the robbers had to look elsewhere.

Up on the Downs, above the village of Collingbourne Kingston, was a small farmhouse where an old couple lived all alone. Once, they'd had a brood of children, but sickness had taken three before they were grown. The surviving two had been sent away due to poverty, one to be a kitchen maid at a big house in Marlborough, and her brother to train as a groom in Pewsey. The old couple were proud that their children had found such good positions, but it left them short on the farm and there was only so much the old man could do. So he'd sold off the farmland piece by piece until there was only a tiny bit left, and now they were very poor.

The couple were well loved in the village. The old woman never had a cross word for anyone, and the old man always found the good in people. So most days you'd see one of the women of the village tramping up the path with an extra loaf, or some leftover apples, or a twist of sugar that'd got a bit damp. They'd stop up there for a gossip, and maybe haul up a little water from the well to save the old woman's back.

One day that winter, the miller's wife was walking up the hill towards the cottage with a spare bag of flour under her arm. The cottage lay in a dip, so you were nearly at the door before you saw it, but the miller's wife was pleased to see, as she approached, a plume of smoke rising from the dip.

'Thank Heaven for that,' she thought. 'It'd be a long way to climb if they weren't in.' But as she got closer it seemed to her that there was far too much smoke, and it didn't smell quite like ordinary fire-smoke should, but of ... other things. She quickened her pace – and then stopped in horror as a gout of smoke filled the sky. She dropped the bag of flour and ran towards the cottage until she could see down into the little valley where it lay.

The cottage was gone. All that remained were smoking ruins. For a moment the miller's wife stood there, shocked by the devastation. Then she turned and ran back to the village. Her shrieks drew the men out of the houses and farms and it wasn't long before a posse was on its way up to the cottage.

The blacksmith was the first to approach. 'I'll make sure it's safe,' he said. 'You're not to come in till I give the word.'

The others watched him duck under the drooping lintel and then they started to search near the charred ruins, calling out the old couple's names.

'You can stop that,' said the blacksmith when he emerged from the cottage.

The villagers turned back. The blacksmith looked older, somehow, than when he'd gone into the house, and it wasn't just because of the ash that covered him. He nodded to the Vicar.

'You'd better come and witness this, Vicar,' he said. 'It's safe enough.'

The Vicar followed the blacksmith inside. There was only the one room, and the Vicar saw almost immediately what the black-smith wanted him to see.

'May the Lord have mercy on their souls,' he whispered. Lying on the cracked flagstones were the remains of the old couple, burnt almost beyond recognition. Almost. The Vicar began to gag.

'Save that till you get outside,' said the blacksmith in a dead voice. 'Come and look at this.'

The Vicar edged around the bodies till he was beside the blacksmith. Together they knelt by the old couple's heads. The Vicar looked where the other man was pointing.

'You see what I see?' said the blacksmith.

'My God!' whispered the Vicar. The old couple hadn't died from the fire. They'd been killed before that; their heads stoved in so hard no burning could disguise it. Just like the men that were sometimes found in shallow graves on the edge of the woods up by the highway.

A hue and cry was raised to search for the robbers. Men came from Collingbourne Kingston, from Collingbourne Ducis, from Everleigh and from Aughton to try to capture the men and take them up to Devizes Gaol so they could be hanged at the next sessions.

The robbers, though, knew the country like the backs of their hands. They were born and bred in Pewsey, both of them, and had worked as farm labourers in the very villages whose people now chased them. They were hard men and used to living rough, and they laughed at the villagers' shouts for their blood.

The robbers dodged here and they dodged there, and for two nights they evaded the villagers by hiding in old farm sheds and ducking into copses while the hue and cry passed by. But by the third night, they'd run as far as they could. They were exhausted, cornered on the Downs between Collingbourne Kingston and Everleigh, and the torches of the villagers drew ever closer. The only cover was the woods that lay below them. There was no cover up on the hills, but no one went into Everleigh Woods at night.

The robbers could hear the shouting, they could see the torches, almost feel the villagers' breath on the back of their necks. They had no choice. So they plunged into the woods. They fought their way through the hazel coppice, tripping over the brambles that snaked between the trees, crying out as branches whipped their faces and vicious barbs snared their ankles, till at last they were in the heart of the wood, the beech trees and the oaks towering high above them. For a moment, they rested, chests heaving. There was no way the men would follow them into the wood. Not with the stories people told about it.

Then they saw it. A torch, not far away – no, two – and burning green, not yellow. The two men looked at each other in alarm and then ran deeper into the wood. But wherever they went, the torches followed. There was no shouting. The bearers of these torches were

silent – you couldn't even hear their feet on the crisp icy ground – though the robbers could hear every crunch their own feet made. It was as if there were no bearers. But the torches shone on.

The robbers ran and ran, and they didn't care that the brambles snagged their legs, and they didn't care that the branches whipped their faces and tore at their hair. For they knew, in their heart of hearts, that it was not villagers that followed them, but something else besides. They remembered the stories now; oh yes, they remembered the stories very well indeed. But if they could just keep running long enough, it wouldn't catch them.

But again they had to rest. With chests heaving, they both leant against a tree and panted, trying to get back their breath. As soon as they looked up they saw it again. Two green lights staring at them, just a pace or two away. By now their eyes had adjusted to the extra darkness of the wood and they saw what followed them.

It was a great black dog. As big as a pony it was, with two burning eyes of green fire. As it watched them it gave a low growl that turned the robbers' bowels to water. As it growled, its hackles rose and exposed long, sharp fangs.

They didn't stay to study it any longer. With screams they couldn't control, they turned to run. As soon as they moved, the dog leapt, and in one bound was right behind them. They crashed back through the undergrowth, not caring where they ran, just running to get away, to get anywhere. But always it was just behind. So close they could feel its breath hot on their necks.

They ran and they ran until the dog chased them out of the woods and into the waiting arms of the hue and cry. As they were clapped in irons, the two robbers looked back to the woods, and there, watching them as they were hauled away, was the black dog, his green eyes burning bright in the darkness.

The robbers were hauled off to Devizes in triumph by the villagers. But when they came to Devizes to watch the hanging, all the villagers would say was, 'We knew we'd have them when they turned into the woods. Everyone knows that the Black Dog lives there, and he can't abide them that has evil in their soul. We knew he'd send them straight out again.'

Black Dogs are a common sight in England, although you'd not want to see one as they are considered a portent of death. There are dozens of accounts of them just in Wiltshire. In her Ghosts and Legends of the Wiltshire Countryside, *Kathleen Wiltshire lists dogs at Wilbury House, the Lacock road, Deane Water Bottom, Abingdon Park Lane in Cricklade, a road near Stourton, the dower-house at Stourhead, Hinton Brook, Coate near Bishop's Cannings, Longbridge Deverill, Crockerton, Black Dog Wood, Black Dog Hill, Quemerford, Preshute Lane, Roundway Down, Toothill, Donhead St Mary, Wilton, a chalkpit near Great Durnford, Ramsbury and Great Oxmoor. They may well be many others. But only the Black Dog of Collingbourne Kingston has been known to do a good deed.*

27

SMILING JACK

Jack was well known in Salisbury as a hawker who was always accompanied by his long-suffering donkey, Ned. He sold the townsfolk milk from the dairy farms and vegetables from the market gardens, and from the town he brought knick-knacks and gee-gaws to the villages and farms. He was well known for his grin, and folk said this was Jack's craft: he'd gull them with laughter and songs into parting with more of their hard-earned cash than they'd intended. They called him 'Smiling Jack', always with a nod or wink or a touch to the eye to show they were canny, that he'd not fool them.

The villagers liked a laugh, and they liked Jack's easy banter. They liked too the town goods he brought them. He was welcome in all the inns for twenty miles around Salisbury and welcome by plenty of fires along the way. More welcome, they said, with that nod or wink again, than he was by his own hearth at Bishopstone. His Betty had waited up too many long nights in vain for her Jack to come home with his earnings, so she was little inclined these days to make life easy for him.

That Whitsuntide, when the May blossom was in full bloom and the Ebble ran at full spate, Jack was asked to preside at a club feast in his own home village of Homington. His old mother had lived there till her death not two years before. Jack knew all the folk and the folk all knew Jack. He was determined that even if the weather was foul he'd be there.

He decked himself up in his very best, from his shiny top hat all the way down to the gleaming spurs on his boots. Ned's ears flicked when he saw the spurs, but he made not a sound when Jack leapt on his back with a loud 'Huzzah!' and dug the nasty things into his hide. Jack imagined himself a hero of great renown and Ned his white shining steed, with ringing bells on his mane and tail. Ned planned revenge for those spurs.

The city was impressed: half of Salisbury turned out to see Jack off with shouts and cheers. 'Where you going, Jack?' everyone called. But Jack was so lost in his dream he didn't say a word. He just let the dust fly up in their faces as he and Ned careered by.

By the time he got onto Bishopstone Hill, above Homington, his dreams had cooled and he remembered poor Ned. He leapt down off Ned's back to lead him up the hill. Usually, Jack was more tender-hearted to his donkey than he was to his wife, which is maybe why Ned was so irked about those spurs and dragged his hooves.

Jack was back on Ned's back when they came into Homington. He paid the toll on the road to John, his old schoolmate, with a joke and commiserations that John would miss the feast. Then he jogged happily down the street as old friends and relations came out to greet him to the sound of the church bells.

Seeing his old friends, Jack realised, with a guilty start, he hadn't been there since his mother died. He turned up his smile a notch and jumped down to shake hands and slap backs and laugh. His friends led him away towards the church.

It was club feast day! Sound the bells and get the men out of their houses, for there was eating and drinking – oh yes, there was drinking – to be done! First though, Jack slipped away from the club dignitaries to tie up Ned at the Fox and Goose and down a chaser to see him through the church service.

After church, the club men led their guest of honour down to the feast. The tables were already groaning with the best food that could be found. There was roast beef, of course, and Wiltshire ham, sausages too, and pies with meat and pies with cheese, tart apples and pickled onions and a round Wiltshire cheese. There was potted chicken and potted ham, twice-roasted tatties, and apple and onion pie and, more important for Jack than anything else, there were quarts and quarts of ale.

To see the villagers and their guest set to would bring a tear to your eye. The food fairly flew off the table and into their mouths. It wasn't often that the villagers had such a fine feast, and they joked that if the men of Homington couldn't put away that beer, then it would hard to imagine who could.

Jack was at the head of them all, cracking jokes and regaling them with stories that made their sides split. The tobacco smoke hung in thicker and thicker layers around them as their voices were raised up in song. The wives, sweethearts and children arrived and soon the young ones were up and dancing.

Jack couldn't remember the last time he'd had such a fine time. He sang and he drank in turn, and by the time the drink had been around a few times he couldn't remember much at all. He certainly wasn't thinking of the five-mile journey home.

At midnight, or just before, Tom the landlord came in and bellowed, 'Your time is up, lads! You'll have to go, else my licence will be lost.'

But everyone begged Jack to oblige them with one last witty verse. Jack tried, but his voice was just a croak. The clapping turned to laughter as he slumped back down on the bench.

'One for the road!' he cried. 'Jus' the one before I go. Tom, bring round my Ned and I'll be on my way.'

Tom passed him another ale without a word and whispered to a lad to fetch the donkey. Then he and Jack's own cousin got their arms under Jack's shoulders and hefted him out the door and up on the donkey's back. Patient Ned, roused from his beauty sleep, was rewarded with a slap on the rump. Down the street he went like a scalded pig, with Jack hanging off him like a sack of potatoes.

At the toll gate, John stepped forward to take his money. Ned wasn't stopping, not for anyone, and Jack had no idea the gate was even there. John shook his fist at their retreating backs, and shouted, 'To the Devil with you! You'll pay double next time around!'

Now Ned had an idea of the way home. Up the hill he plodded. He put up with the snoring dead weight of his master on his back. It was clear to him that his master had had more than a glass. But Ned only knew so much of the way, and Jack was in no fit state to guide him, so when Ned saw an easy path downhill he took it.

Eventually it dawned on Jack that the land didn't look quite right. He gave a sharp tug on the reins. Ned started and set his teeth. Enough was enough. First spurs and now this! He bucked, and pitched his master to the ground. Jack landed with a splash in the water meadows.

'The river?' cried Jack, realising where they were. 'Ah, Ned, how'd we get down by the Ebble?'

Suddenly a light appeared in the darkness, and then a ghostly form flitted in front of Jack's wondering eyes.

'It's just the drink,' he muttered to himself. 'What would a will-o'-the-wisp want with me?'

Clouds were gathering in the night sky. They smothered up the moon until it was so dark that Jack could hardly see his hand in front of his face. Thunder cracked and lightning flashed. Jack looked up when the thunder cracked, and there in the flash of lightning he saw Old Nick himself, stood right in front of him with his horns all polished and his leathery skin shining red and his forked tail a-swishing.

He beckoned to Jack to follow him.

Jack felt one foot rise and then the other, and he found himself pulled, step after step, towards the fiend. Right then Ned let out a terrified eeee-ore as he caught sight of the fiend. Jack snapped out of the enchantment and tried to bolt instead, but his legs seemed stuck fast in the boggy water.

Ned brayed in terror as he too found his legs wouldn't work. Jack fell to his knees in the mud and began to pray. He swore him blind and swore him blue that he would never touch a drop of liquor again, nor worry his dear, good Betty. The rain started, thick, heavy, soaking drops, but Jack hardly felt them as he prayed. But for a full half hour he couldn't move his limbs as the Devil flitted all around him, laughing and crying out for his soul.

At last, the rain began to ease. Both Jack and Ned were released, and Jack fell flat on his face in the water. When he hauled himself up, spluttering, he was just in time to see Old Nick give a hiss and vanish under the ground.

Jack didn't waste a moment. He called for Ned, sprang on his back, and off they set as fast as Ned could go with Jack hanging onto his ears. The brambles tore at them, the branches whipped them, but Ned wasn't stopping. They came up by the walls of Throope Manor, and Ned sprinted round them as if the hounds of Hell were after him. Neither Jack nor Ned looked round, just in case they were. When they reached the stream, Ned was still so afraid that he leapt it in one bound and was away on the other side and heading home. He didn't stop until he was trembling outside his owner's door.

Only thing was, Jack wasn't with him. Ned had taken such a high leap he'd pitched his master in the stream. Jack, meanwhile, hauled himself out of the brook and cursed his donkey. But that took all of his strength. When he stood up to walk the short way home, his head spun and he fell down insensible in the stream.

Betty, waiting up back in Bishopstone, drained her cup of tea and set it down with a click. 'I've waited up long enough,' she said to the empty air. 'He's drunk a pint or two too many. I suppose it'll be the morning before I see him.'

The next morning, though, Jack wasn't in bed. When Betty opened the front door, she saw poor Ned standing there all alone.

'Where's your master?' she cried. 'Have you left him?'

Ned shook his head and brayed a piteous bray.

Betty raised the hue and cry, and the men of the village set out in all directions to search for him, calling out, 'Smiling Jack! Smiling Jack!' Betty wept and wailed to the other women that she'd have to wear the widow's weeds, and that Jack was the best of husbands – kind and true, if a little fond of the liquor.

Just as she was working up a terrible din, there came a shout from the road. There was Tom Bawter, leading his trap, with Jack spread-eagled pale and bloody in the back. Betty gave a shriek – and Jack bolted upright. He looked around and saw the whole village staring back at him. So he leapt off the trap and ran indoors. The villagers' laughter followed him up the stairs and under the bedclothes.

But Jack was none the worse for wear from his adventure. He even kept his word and never let strong liquor pass his lips again. He still smiled and joked, but now the joke was on him. Everyone knew about how Smiling Jack had dined and supped at Homington Club so long that the Devil had appeared. Jack laughed too, but despite his laughter he never went back over Bishopstone Hill at night again, and he steered clear of the water-meadows, and more than anything he made sure he was always especially nice to Ned.

This story is another one taken from Edward Slow's verse. It depicts the area around Salisbury that Slow knew so well and whose accent he preserved in writing.

28

St Aldhelm

Centwin of Wessex stepped out of the church and blinked in the bright sunlight. His wife Engyth followed him and stopped to stare at her husband standing there so distracted.

'Husband? What's wrong?' She laid a gentle hand on his arm.

Centwin looked down for a moment and seemed startled to see her there, but his eyes were quickly drawn back to where the boundary of the churchyard was marked by a tall stone cross.

'Come with me.' Taking his wife's hand, he led her across the churchyard to the stone. They stared at the saints carved on it: John the Baptist clutching a lamb; Paul and Anthony breaking bread in the desert; Mary Magdalene washing Christ's feet. The cross was covered in ornate carvings. As Engyth watched, the vine leaves intertwined around the stone figures seemed to writhe and dance in the sunlight.

Then something struck her in the belly. For a moment she was caught in the pain piercing through her, but it soon passed. When she looked up there was nothing strange to be seen. The cross stood still and quiet. The sun was now obscured behind a cloud.

The couple thought nothing of it. But three months later, Engyth told Centwin that she was with child. The baby was a healthy boy, and they named him Aldhelm. He was born almost exactly nine months after the day in the churchyard. Engyth wondered what God had in store for him. But she kept her thoughts to herself, and the boy began to learn what he needed to know to be a noble Saxon lord.

But the will of God was not to be ignored. Engyth was a pious woman and took her small son to church every week. One time, when Aldhelm was no more than three, as the priest droned his way through the liturgy as he did every week and the congregation dozed, little Aldhelm sat as if transfixed. Then, up in the roof, there was a tweeting and a twittering. People jerked out of their snoozing and looked up. The roof was filled with tiny birds, all singing their hearts out. As the congregation watched, the birds flew down and settled on Aldhelm's shoulders and head. They picked at his hair and sang as he chuckled and stroked their feathers.

After that, his parents knew he was best suited to the Church. As soon as he was old enough he was sent to the best church school in the land, far away from Wessex. He was put in the care of the highest priest of England, the Archbishop of Canterbury. At St Augustine's in Canterbury, Aldhelm flourished. He learnt Greek and Latin with a speed that almost frightened his tutors. But he was lonely, and he thought often of the rolling hills of Wessex and wished he could go home and learn there.

As soon as he had completed his schooling, he left Canterbury. He visited his family, of course, but there was something else that drew him back west. A new community had been founded at Malmesbury, and the churchmen in Canterbury were both angry and excited. Rumours whirled about this Maildubh, this Irishman who had come to bring a different vision of Christ to the people of Wessex. Aldhelm couldn't resist the lure. Wasn't this exactly what he had wanted? He had to go and see for himself.

He was impressed by what he saw and heard at Malmesbury, and he longed to stay with Maildubh and learn everything he had to teach. Abbot Maildubh, for his part, was a cunning man and he saw in Aldhelm great things for the future. He allowed Aldhelm to stay for a while, and watched him as the younger man gobbled up all that Malidubh had to teach him and came back begging for more. Maildubh tested Aldhelm with questions and riddles, and when he was satisfied with the young man's answers, he sent him back to Canterbury.

'Learn all you can there,' he said. 'When you have exhausted their learning, come back to me.'

Although he didn't want to go, Aldhelm knew that obedience was expected of him by Malidubh – and by God. He returned, but when he got there he found that a new teacher had come to Canterbury. For a year and a day he sat at the feet of Adrian the African and learnt all he could, and then he went back to Malmesbury. But when he arrived he found that Malidubh was ill.

'You have learnt well,' said Maildubh. 'You have learnt enough to start a new journey. You will be Abbot after me.'

Soon after, Maildubh died and Aldhelm was made Abbot. He mourned his mentor, but he soon found that he had plenty of ideas of his own. First, he looked at the old church that Maildubh had chosen as the site for the monastery. Barely ten people could squash inside it, and already some of the monks had to stand outside to hear the words of the priest inside. A new church was needed, one that would put Malmesbury on the map.

Aldhelm had money and royal connections. The only problem was that there was no good building stone. Mostly, people had ransacked the old city of giants at Bath or raided the fallen ruins that lay around the countryside, great estates once but now gone to waste. But those stocks were drying up, and the stone was old and no longer strong. There was no new stone for building.

But Aldhelm was determined. At first it seemed hopeless. He searched and searched, but there was no good stone to be had. But Aldhelm refused to be downhearted. After many days of searching and disappointment he was riding at Hazelbury, near Box, and he felt a sudden urge to stop. Immediately he threw down his glove.

'Dig here!' he commanded his men. 'There is great treasure to be found!'

His men, imagining gold and silver, hurried to dig. But it was a greater treasure than that. As they dug, a pale, smooth stone was revealed under a thin covering of earth. They had discovered the finest stone beds that they had ever seen, the finest stone to make the finest church in Wessex.

Aldhelm threw himself into the building work, too, for he soon found that things went wrong if he didn't keep a careful eye on them. One time, the carpenters came to him with their heads hung low.

'Those timbers we ordered, you know, for the roof. Well ... one's too short.'

'Show me,' commanded Aldhelm, and, sure enough, when he arrived on the scene he saw that one huge log was a lot shorter than the others.

Aldhelm stood over the log and raised his hands.

The men who had delivered the timber fell to their knees, expecting punishment. Instead, the log grew, and grew, and grew until it was exactly the length of the others.

So Aldhelm's fame grew. Some say he even caused the bells to ring to silence the thunder if a storm brewed up when a service was taking place. He built more churches – at Frome and at Bradford on Avon. But he remained humble. When he felt that he thought too much about earthly things, he went out to a spring on the hill near the church to stand in the cold water.

But it was his teaching that drew people. They flocked from all around to hear him speak. Aldhelm realised that to teach people was what he had truly been called to do. He went out to the stone crosses that marked the boundaries between parishes and stood at the entrances to churches. These crosses were carved with scenes from the Good Book. Word would go out that a saint was there to talk to the people. The villagers would come. Some were equipped with rotten vegetables and eggs in case they didn't like what they heard. But Aldhelm was ready. Instead of preaching, he told them stories. He clowned, even juggled if it made them listen. And he sang so sweetly that all the little birds would come and listen as well.

One time he was preaching near Warminster with a huge crowd around him. They were listening but became restless when a fine drizzle began to fall. Aldhelm knew the signs – the shuffling feet, the muttering, the looking this way and that – and got out his juggling balls, thrust his staff into the ground behind him to keep it out of the way and began his usual tricks to win back the people's attention. At first, he was caught up in what he was doing – this ball in the hand like so, as the next rises and the third is flying – but he soon realised the people were paying him no attention at all. They were staring right behind him. When he turned around he saw why.

His staff had taken root and transformed into a great ash tree of a hundred branches.

Aldhelm fell to his knees and worshipped God there and then, and the people followed him. The tree flourished and grew, and from it many saplings grew, and the place came to be known as 'Bishopstrow' – the place of the Bishop's Tree.

Aldhelm's fame spread far and wide. It even reached Pope Sergius in Rome. Sergius was suspicious of this foreign bishop and decided to test him. He sent word that Aldhelm was to visit him, but there was a catch. Aldhelm was to arrive in Rome two days after he received the message. In those days, a journey to Rome would take months, through hazardous and difficult country. Aldhelm knew that, but he understood the test.

He went into the church and lifting his fine singing voice to the rafters, he called out to God to help him. From out of the air came spirits, bright-eyed, flitting things that drifted on the air beside him.

Aldhelm asked the first, 'How fast can you go?'

'As fast as a bird,' it cried. But that wasn't quick enough.

He turned to the second and asked, 'How fast can you go?

'As fast as an arrow.' But that wasn't quick enough either.

'How fast can you go?' Aldhelm asked the third.

'As fast as thought,' it answered, and that was fast enough.

He commanded that the spirit take the shape of a great horse, and then he mounted his spirit steed. He was at the gates of Rome in a flash.

The Pope, impressed, allowed Aldhelm to preach in the city. Soon the people of Rome were flocking to hear the preaching of a man who juggled and sang and told them stories. Aldhelm was happy in Rome, but while he was there a great scandal brewed up which threatened the Pope himself.

A baby was born in the household of the Pope's chamberlain, and the rumour ran around the city that the child was the son of a nun and the Pope. When the child was nine days old, Aldhelm heard word of this. He went straight to the chamberlain's house, took the baby in his arms and carried him to St Peter's, the greatest church in Rome, to baptise him.

Then, jiggling the child, he asked him, 'Are the rumours true? Is the Pope your father?'

The child looked up at Aldhelm and in a high, clear voice declared, 'The Pope is pure and unspotted with shame. He is not my father.'

The Pope was full of gratitude and gave Aldhelm all manner of riches. But it is all very well to have one who protects your reputation, but it is another to have a miracle worker who might steal your own fame. The Pope began to think that it might be best if Aldhelm was safely back in his distant northern land again. He sent Aldhelm home.

This time Aldhelm went the long way, over the Alps. The way really was very long, and the camels the Pope had given him were not strong. One broke its back carrying a great slab of stone – and the stone smashed too, a carved altar frontal that was a personal gift from the Pope. Aldhelm fixed them both, but he quickly got rid of the camels and sent them back to Italy. After that he used good, strong donkeys.

When he got home, he was made Bishop of Sherborne and had to spend most of his time away from his beloved Malmesbury. But he visited when he could, and the church flourished with his favour. But by now, Aldhelm was an old man.

One night, his friend, Egwin, the Bishop of Worcester, had a dream. When he awoke, there were tears in his eyes because he knew that Aldhelm was dead. He knew, too, where he had died and left immediately to fetch the body back from where it lay at Doulting in Somerset. The coffin was processed across the land and every seven miles a cross was planted in honour of the saint.

The monks of Malmesbury came out to greet their old Abbot one last time, and he was buried with great ceremony in the church that he had built. But being dead didn't stop him. Aldhelm continued to work miracles from the grave. His feast day is still celebrated every 25 May, and the spring where he stood in the chill water still runs fresh and cold today.

St Aldhelm is Wiltshire's most famous saint, born in the seventh century at just the time when Christianity was taking hold among the Saxons. There was rivalry between the Church of Rome, based in Canterbury, and the Celtic church that still survived in Wales, Scotland, Cornwall and especially in Ireland. Many Irish monks came to England to convert the pagans and to bring them their kind of Christianity, so Maildubh was not unusual. What is unusual is that Aldhelm, studying at Canterbury, should also be influenced by an Irish monk.

29

THE AMESBURY ARCHER

The boy was born in the shadow of the high mountains. He learnt to swim in the chill mountain lakes, jumping off the platform around his mother's house with the other boys to swim among the fish. He roamed the high passes with the goats and lay in meadows thick with wild flowers. He ate plump venison and thin flatbread and ran out with a birchbark basket to gather tiny alpine strawberries and fat blackberries. He was hardly more than a baby when a bow was placed in his hands. His brothers and cousins showed him how to pull back the string, first against the face, and then, as he grew stronger, against the shoulder. He started by hunting the hares that ran on the grassy slopes. Later, he went with the young men hunting red deer.

He loved the thrill of the chase, running through the thick forests and out onto the meadows He loved the scent of sweat and fear and the pull and snap of the bowstring and the feasting with his brothers. But another path was mapped for him. His father was a traveller who had walked into the village as a young man with stories to tell and skills to sell. He had caught the eye of a village girl and had settled. He still had an itch to travel, but his skill made him precious. Too precious to let go.

For the young archer's father was a magician. He used the magic in fire to make things of beauty from stones dug from the ground. Hidden inside the stones were seams of gleaming metal. Once extracted, by the alchemy of fire the metal could be hammered into things of beauty and power. The young archer learnt his father's secrets and had a flair for working the metal that his elder brothers lacked. His father poured all his hopes into this youngest son, and the young archer knew from an early age that he would be the one to continue his father's work and pass the knowledge of the spirits of fire and metal on in his turn.

Fire and heat give the spirits power, his father told him. 'There's power in working with the spirits, but there is responsibility too. You must go, find new seams of the metal and bring the magic to the people you meet. You'll be a man of power to them. Don't do what I did, and get snared by good land and beautiful women. Women stay where they are – they are part of a place. You must go and spread your seed so that more smiths are born, and you must teach the sons of the villages your skill. Keep walking, and don't settle.'

So the young man learnt to work with the spirits to turn the copper into shining knives. They weren't as useful as the stone ones that everyone used, but they were things of such beauty that a man would trade a horse to have one. And then there was gold. It was magic all by itself. Every time he handled it, that metal tingled in his hands and filled him with awe. It never tarnished, it was more unchanging than the spirits, and those who carried it to their graves bought a piece of eternity that would bring them luck and power in the land of the ancestors.

The young man never stopped practising with his bow, and so the people of his village took to calling him 'the Archer'. But though he still took pleasure in running with the deer in the mountains, he itched to leave. And when his father spoke to him about foreign women, well, that only spurred on his desire to begin his journeying.

The day came at last when his father deemed him ready to leave. In a secret ceremony, the Archer pledged himself to the spirits of fire and of metal, pledged that he would spread his seed and

teach the craft. When that was done, and his goodbyes were said, he strapped his bow on his back, tied on his stone wrist-guards, packed up his cushion stone for working the metal and then turned his back on the mountains and set out the way the wind pulled him. To the west.

He travelled out of the mountains and down into a thickly forested land spiked with strange pinnacles of rock and cut with deep ravines. He crossed mysterious deep hollows sunk in the land and visited each village he came upon. As he had promised, he shared his knowledge and spread his seed. It was a good time, but after a while he found it harder to leave places. The further he walked from the mountains, the lonelier he became.

He wanted more than this trekking from place to place. And in one place, a deep wooded valley with a trout-filled river, he met a woman who welcomed him not as a stranger but as a friend and a lover. Although he remembered his father's words, when he

travelled on he was no longer alone. The woman walked by his
side. He worried that he had broken his pledge as a smith, but he
loved her and she him and that was the end of it.

The two of them walked until there was no more land and ahead
of them stretched the grey sea. The Archer had never seen anything
of such power as this. It made him afraid and he was all for turning
south, but his wife shook her head and laid a hand on the gentle
swell of her belly.

'There is a land across the water,' she said, 'that they say is filled
with power. There's a powerful temple in the centre of the island.
The spirits are strong there and the ancestors watch over the
people.' But as far as she knew, the islanders didn't have the magic
the Archer had. 'Take your magic to the temple,' she said. 'Our
child will be born in a place of power. He or she will be strong.'

They found a man who could speak to the spirits of the sea and
asked him to take them across in his log boat. The Archer felt fear
as he stepped into the boat and handed over a precious copper
knife as payment, but the crossing was smooth. When they landed,
they asked about the temple in the centre of island, and were told
that this was a land of many temples. It seemed to be a land in
which people became priests simply by dwelling in the land. They
were told that many came to visit the temples and study with the
priests. They were led to a trackway that stretched across the land.
'This will take you to the place of the temples,' they were told.

From this ridgeway they saw that land. She was a gentle land,
with rolling bare-topped hills. Thick woods grew in the valleys.
Sheep and cattle cropped the grassy slopes. They saw villages and
their small fields of hop bines and waving wheat. Fat red deer fell
under the Archer's bow, and they traded the venison for bread heavy
with seeds. They guessed that in the autumn the apples would be
tart and the berries sweet and the beer brewed to mellowness. She
was a welcoming land.

Looking down from the ridge, they saw at last, down on the
rolling plain, the greatest of the temples. Great earthworks
serpented across the plains. They saw circles of wooden posts
within the earthworks, decorated with fetishes and paint and

blood, and they shivered as they sensed the power of the ancestors. The Archer felt foolish at the thought of offering his own small power, but it was all he had.

He need not have feared. It was the priests who were afraid. They'd heard of this magic, but in truth they had hardly believed what they had heard, that fire could shape metal and create things of beauty.

'Such a powerful magic will only bring change and trouble,' they said. They wondered if they should turn him away. But they knew that if they did not welcome him and his magic, then others would. So the Archer settled there with his wife and taught the people at the temple his craft. Again, he worried that he was breaking his pledge. But he wanted to settle, he had walked far enough, and he wanted his new son to grow up in this fine place and be a part of this land.

A few years later, when his first son had a brother and a sister, the Archer heard that a group of people had come from the west to visit the temples and to share their own knowledge of the spirits. This family was led by a priest and he spoke of stones.

'Stones,' he said, 'are for the ancestors, whereas wood, living wood, is for life.'

He said that healing flowed through the stones from the ancestors to the living. At first the priests laughed, but the people listened. The Archer was caught up in the stranger priest's description of the blue stones that gave healing in his own land that lay to the west, among low sweeping mountains sheltered in mist.

The priest's prestige grew as it was revealed that some of his men had the same metalworking magic as the Archer. The Archer was drawn to the priest and his family, whose lives seemed to echo his own. His support lent weight to the western priest's arguments, and the priests of the place started to listen. Together they made plans for a whole new complex of stone and wood temples by the river.

When he wasn't planning to change the world, the Archer went hunting with the priest and his cousins. Together they shot red deer to get the sacred antler picks that were needed to dig the holes in which the new stones would be placed.

When it was time, the Archer went with the priest and his cousins and many others to fetch the stones. The priest said there had never been a venture like this before, with so many people working together to venerate the spirits of the ancestors. They would be blessed and the land would be grateful and be bountiful for them.

The short journey to the west seemed to the Archer to be the culmination of all his journeying. When they came to the high blue stone circle beside a cairn in the ragged hills of the west, he fell down on his knees in awe. They cut from the hills more of that fine blue stone and rolled the huge boulders down to the river. They shunted them onto the waiting rafts and then they were off on the wild sea and around the rocky coast of the great island. They came back through the broad estuary that ran up into the north, testing all the while for mudflats that would ground them. The local people were proud to help them and be part of it. As they travelled, word spread and many joined them to attend the ceremonies that would consecrate the circles.

From the estuary they turned into a river running east. Soon after they joined that river the Archer's luck ran out. As they came through the crashing rocks and high ravines of a gorge, his raft was caught by the rocks. With the burden of heavy stone, it was impossible to steer; the raft swung wide, the stone slid and crashed into the swift running water. The raft tipped up and pitched everyone on it into the water.

That stone was lost, but people on the banks dragged the Archer and the priest from the water. The Archer survived to return to his family, but his travelling days were done. While the young men dug the sacred holes with antler picks from the red deer he had once hunted, the Archer lay on his bed at home wracked with a raging fever and despairing over his ruined knee. The pain never left him. Even the new healing stones could do little for him. The priest got off more lightly. With only a broken hip, he healed well enough, and thereafter gave thanks to the stones every day. He couldn't understand why they hadn't worked for the Archer. But the Archer remembered his broken pledge to the spirits of fire and metal, and he understood.

He could still work the copper and, though he could no longer travel, more people than ever flocked to the temples and the Archer shared his metal craft with them all. It was an exciting time to be alive. The Archer clung to life and took joy in his friends and family.

But one last challenge awaited him. Sickness came. A new sickness that the stones could not heal. The priests worked harder than ever to placate the spirits, but many died.

The Archer died, as did his eldest son. The priest conducted his friend's funeral. First, there was feasting near the wooden circles at the place of the living. Then the Archer was carried west to the river, for rebirth into the realm of the ancestors. Then they carried him north, up a wide avenue towards the place of the dead where the blue stones stood. After the ceremony, he and his son were buried alongside each other in all their finery. The priest placed beaker pots at the Archer's head and feet and laid his tools around him. Into his hair he clipped untarnishing gold hair ornaments. Of course, the Archer took his copper knives with him, and the priest's cousins, who remembered hunting the sacred red deer, placed arrowhead after arrowhead upon his body.

'The Archer walks straight and tall among the ancestors now,' said the priest. 'His hand will guide the bow of the hunter, and it will guide the hand of the smith.'

So it was for many years. The Archer's hand guided the bronze smith, the blacksmith, the ironworker. Throughout long ages, Stonehenge remained a place of power, even when its original purpose was forgotten. But in the end the Archer was forgotten. His quiet sleep under the earth went undisturbed. Then, in 2002, a housing scheme was planned on Boscombe Down near Amesbury. The archaeologists came to check the land and the Archer was found once more. Immediately the story of the Archer spread. They called him the King of Stonehenge. His story was told on the radio, on television and on the internet. When the housing estate was finished, the school was named after the Archer, which seems entirely fitting for one who taught all his life.

This story has been constructed around the two famous burials near Stonehenge excavated by Wessex Archaeology in 2002 and 2003: the Amesbury Archer and the Boscombe Bowmen. Of course, the story is a fantasy, but there are portions of truth in it. The place of the living is Woodhenge, on the outskirts of Amesbury, and the place of the dead is, of course, Stonehenge. From studies of the Archer's tooth enamel it is thought he came from somewhere in Central Europe, possibly Switzerland or Austria, and that the Bowmen came from either Brittany or Wales – possibly from the very Preseli Hills from which the blue stones at Stonehenge came. A crescent of blue stones was the first stonework at Stonehenge, the sarsen-stone triathlons following soon after. The burials both date from around 2500-2200 BC, and coincide not only with the building works at Stonehenge that saw the structure take the shape we know today, but also with the arrival of metalworking in copper. This copper-working 'Beaker' culture heralds the beginning of the Bronze Age in Britain. The Archer and the Bowmen may have seen any of the stages of construction in that period, from the crescent of blue stones to the erection of the great sarsen-stones, but we will never know if they had anything to do with Stonehenge's construction, just as we will never know for sure what rites took place there and what these people believed. But that doesn't stop us imagining that the Archer and the Bowmen must have been men of power.

30

THE FAIRIES OF
HACKPEN HILL

Ambrose was a shepherd from Winterbourne Bassett and he loved his job. He loved it not so much because of the sheep, though he took good care of them and guarded them well, but because taking the sheep out allowed him to be in the place he loved: the Downs.

The Downs were Ambrose's life. He loved them in every season. He loved to lie on the damp grass on a spring morning with the cowslips and the long purples around him and watch the clouds scudding through the watery blue sky. He loved to listen to the high tweedling of the lark and squint into the sun trying to see it. He loved the round hills and the beech copses, and he even loved to sit out on the Downs on a cold winter's night and watch the snowflakes swirling round his lantern while sheep bleated in the darkness.

The other thing he loved was his fiddle. It made him popular at the inns, and he was often called to weddings and christenings to play a lively tune. But what he loved most was to take the fiddle up on the Downs with his sheep. He'd play the song of the lark and the brightness of the spring flowers. He played the wild winds that shuddered over the ridges and whistled up the valleys. He played the sunshine and the rain, the snow and the crisp frosty grass, and the sheep would gather round to listen.

One night, while watching his sheep and playing the clouds as they scudded over the moon and lit a corona round it, he became so involved in his fiddle-playing that he didn't look up for a long time. When at last he did, he found all his sheep had gone. He jumped to his feet and stared wildly around in search of them. It seemed that his flock of a hundred had disappeared into thin air.

Grabbing his fiddle, he frantically scrambled up and down the hills, calling out their names, but they were nowhere to be found. Could they really have been rustled right from under his nose? But then he looked up, and there on the ridge top, he caught a glimpse of something white. Not his sheep, but something so white that it glowed as bright as the moon. He squinted up at it, and sucked in his breath. It was a deer, a white hind, and behind her marched his sheep.

Ambrose scrambled quickly up the hill and fell in behind them. They were ambling slowly along, but nothing he said would make them come. Even pulling them away didn't work, for as soon as he let go the sheep would shake itself and then trot quickly until it was back in line. So Ambrose ran on to the front where the deer led the troop. The animal gave off such a bright light that he couldn't make out what lay behind her, and had to shield his eyes. But as he drew closer, she disappeared. For a moment he couldn't see, but then his eyes adjusted and he stopped dead.

In front of him was the familiar hump shape of a barrow. He was on Hackpen Hill, above the village, where a line of the fell mounds lay scattered across the hill. Many a day he'd sheltered behind a barrow in the lee of the wind, but in the dark the crumpled entrance had become a yawning maw of damp earth and crumbling stones. And into it filed his sheep. One by one they went, as if in some trance or dream.

Ambrose trembled. He knew what lived inside the barrows and knew that his fellows who worked in the village would think him bold just to have dozed against one for an hour on a sunny day. But the barrow by day was one thing. This uncanny sight was another.

Hesitantly he inched closer, but he froze again at the entrance and the sheep simply brushed past him as if he was not there.

For a long minute he stood there, wondering what to do. If he went down to the village tomorrow without the sheep and spun some tale about an enchanted barrow, he'd never work again. He was only a hired hand. He had no land of his own. Losing his sheep – his livelihood – would be a disaster.

Then, as he stood there, he realised what he could do. He still had his fiddle. The sheep loved music. Surely that would bring them back to him? So he set the fiddle to his chin and began to play. He played the lively tunes the sheep enjoyed, and the mournful tunes he himself loved, but the sheep paid no attention. Soon he watched the last one disappear into the darkness.

He had to get the sheep back.

Setting the fiddle back under his chin, he stepped into the tunnel and played as he walked. At first, the light of the moon outside lit his way and reflected off the white chalk of the tunnel. He saw the straggling roots of the plants penetrating though the chalk above him, and felt the chill of dank earth around him.

Soon, though, the light faded until he could hardly see and he was left with just the sound of his own music to guide him on.

But he didn't feel entirely alone. As he walked, he felt something brush his sleeve – a touch like a lady's soft hand – and he shivered. In the last shreds of the light he glimpsed a slight form right beside him, just like the line of a nose and lips, then it dissolved into darkness.

He stumbled as fabric brushed around his legs as if someone passed in full skirts. There was a touch to his face, and the warmth of breath on his cheek, and there, audible over the fiddle, a giggle.

As he walked deeper in, playing all the while, a new light began to grow ahead of him and the ghostly shapes began to solidify into dancers who whirled to his fiddle tunes and laughed as they danced. As the light grew, the tunnel widened out. Ambrose's mouth dropped open and his fiddle fell silent. The tunnel opened into a huge chamber. If it was a chamber – it was so large that he could barely see across it. Above him hung a million lights, like stars in the night sky, but constellations the like of which he had never seen. All around the edge was a forest of buttressed trees. Lights flickered in there – fireflies and the eyes of strange animals that peered at him from the branches. Between the eaves of the forest spread a huge meadow in which uncanny blooms stretched their petals to the spangled night sky and filled the air with sweet perfume. In the meadow danced a thousand people and more, each as beautiful as the next, strange and remote in their beauty. And in front of the trees musicians played. Their tunes were strange and their viols and lutes antique, the kind of thing Ambrose's grandfather might have played.

The music set his feet moving and carried him in among the dancers. They welcomed him with smiles, and soon all he knew was the dance, the music and the laughter of the beautiful ones with whom he danced. How long he danced he did not know. It could have been a moment, it could have been forever.

But then the music faltered. Ambrose looked up as if in a dream and there, walking through the throng, was the most beautiful woman he had ever seen. When she reached him, she smiled, and Ambrose felt his heart melt. He knew as soon as he saw her that he would do anything for her. He yearned towards her, willing her to notice him. Then, as she passed, she turned and smiled and beckoned him to follow.

The music stopped altogether, and suddenly Ambrose remembered who he was and why he was there. His sheep! Hardly knowing what he was doing, he set his fiddle to his chin again

and he began to play. Soon the people around were clapping
their hands in delight and dancing to the jigs and reels he played.
Ambrose, his mind now clear, followed the woman and the crowds
parted to let them pass.

The woman reached the end of the meadow and settled on
a low mound scattered with bright white flowers that echoed
the stars above. She was so beautiful and, as she smiled at him,
Ambrose felt his nerve falter. Did he really want to leave? Surely
it would be better to stay and dance and make music with these
people? Wouldn't it be better to stay with her, the most lovely of
them all?

She smiled as if she knew what he was thinking and beckoned
him yet closer. As he approached, he heard a familiar sound over
the music of his fiddle: the bleat of a sheep. There, beyond the little
mound on which she sat, were his sheep, munching the rich grass.
As soon as he saw them, he realised that he would have to go. This
wasn't his place, and neither was it his sheep's. He paused to look
around at the trees, the lights and the beautiful lady, and felt his
heart shrink. But it had to be done. Without stopping playing, he
nodded his thanks to the Queen and scrambled up over the hill to
the sheep.

They crowded around him, bleating and jostling to get close.
He pushed his way through them to the front, still playing, and
saw that another tunnel lay ahead of him, and he smelt the raw
damp earth of the mortal world. Not daring another look back, he
walked into the tunnel and led the sheep through it, playing all the
while until he stumbled out into the moonlight.

After that, Ambrose was not the same. He hardly ate and seemed
to be wasting away before the villagers' eyes, and if they spoke to
him, he rarely answered, but seemed to stare at something far off
in the distance. He still cared for his sheep, but he never played his
fiddle again. And yet he still took it with him every day up on the
Downs. Some who saw him there said he haunted the barrows as if
he was searching for something. He would stay up there all night as
well, volunteering to take the nightshift from the other shepherds,
and prowl the hill staring up at the ridgeline, and hoping.

Finally one night, as he trudged up Hackpen Hill, he caught a flash of white, and there was the white hind, and he followed. Ambrose was never seen again in Winterbourne Bassett, but who's to say he isn't playing his fiddle to this day underneath Hackpen Hill?

The bare bones of this tale were collected in 1645 by John Aubrey. He met an old man who told of a shepherd from Winterbourne Bassett who strayed into a round barrow but found his way out. There are many tales of people straying into fairyland, and the story goes all the way back to the ancient Greek hero Orpheus searching for Eurydice and further still to the Sumerian goddess Innana seeking her lover in the underworld. As ancient graves, round barrows were obvious entrances to the otherworld where the fairy folk lived. But, like Ambrose, most who go to fairyland and then escape spend the rest of their lives longing to return.

BIBLIOGRAPHY

Ackerman, John Yonge, *Wiltshire Tales* (John Russell Smith: London,1853)

Barber, Richard, *Myths and Legends of the British Isles* (Boydell Press: Woodbridge, 1999)

Briggs, Katherine, *A Dictionary of British Folk Tales in the English Language* (Indiana University Press: Bloomington, 1971)

Bruce, Sir Michael, *Tramp Royal* (Pan: London, 1957)

Burridge, Neil, 'A Woman's Burial from Wessex', http://www.templeresearch.eclipse.co.uk/bronze/wessex_b.htm

Chandler, John and Goodhugh, Peter, *Amesbury: History and Description of a South Wiltshire Town* (The Amesbury Society: Salisbury, 1989)

Egerton, Revd John Coker, *Sussex Folk and Sussex Ways: Stray Studies in the Wealden Formation of Human Nature* (Chatto & Windus: London, 1892)

Garrard, Bruce, *The Arrow: The Founding of the New Cathedral at Salisbury* (Bruce Garrard: Salisbury, 1980)

Geoffrey of Monmouth, *The History of the Kings of Britain*, trans. Lewis Thorpe (Penguin: London, 1966)

Giles, J.A., *William of Malmesbury's Chronicle of the King's of England* (Henry G. Boiin: London, 1867)

Ford, David Nash, *Early British Kingdoms*, http://www.earlybritishkingdoms.com

Hicks, Carola, *Improper Pursuits: The Scandalous Life of Lady Diana Beauclerk* (Pan: London, 2002)

Hutton, Edward, *Highways and Byways in Wiltshire* (MacMillan & Co.: London, 1919)

Jordan, Katharine, *The Folklore of Ancient Wiltshire* (Wiltshire County Council, Library & Museum Service: Trowbridge, 1990)

Jordan, Katy, *The Haunted Landscape: Folklore, Ghosts and Legends of Wiltshire* (Ex Libris Press: Bradford on Avon, 2000)

Malory, Sir Thomas, *Le Morte d'Arthur*, ed. Janet Cowen (Penguin: London, 1969)

Newton, Air Vice-Marshall Barry, 'Airman's Cross', *The Journal of the Royal Air Force Historical Society*, vol. 16, pp. 104-110

Pitts, Mike, *Hengeworld* (Arrow: London, 2001)

Reeves, Les, *The Moonrakers: A Collection of Information about This Famous Legend* (Elare Booklets, 1998)

Slow, Edward, *Figgetty Pooden*, ed. John Chandler (Wiltshire Library & Museum Service: Trowbridge, 1982)

Timbs, John, *Abbeys, Castles and Ancient Halls of England and Wales: Their Legendary Lore and Popular History*, ed. Alexander Gunn (Frederick Warne: London, 1872)

Westwood, Jennifer and Simpson, Jacqueline, *The Lore of the Land: A Guide to England's Legends, from Spring-Heeled Jack to the Witches of Warboys* (Penguin: London, 2005)

Wessex Archaeology, http://www.wessexarch.co.uk/projects/amesbury/archer.html

Whitlock, Ralph, *Wiltshire Folklore and Legends* (Robert Hale: London, 1992)

Williams, Alfred, *A Wiltshire Village* (Duckworth: London, 1920)

Williams, Alfred, *Round About the Upper Thames* (Duckworth: London, 1922)

Wiltshire, Kathleen, *Ghosts & Legends of the Wiltshire Countryside* (Compton Russell: Salisbury, 1973)

Wiltshire, Kathleen, *Wiltshire Folklore* (Compton Russell: Salisbury, 1975)

INDEX